Essentials for the Improvist

Building A Functional Understanding of Arpeggios

Also in this series for advanced players:
Guitar Scales
Guitar Triads

Beginner Series:
Guitar Essentials - Book 1
Guitar Essentials - Book 2

Cover Design: Myles English

Content: Lloyd English

All rights reserved. No part of this book may be reproduced in any form or by any electronic or mechanical means known now or used in the future including and not limited to information and retrieval systems by any and all means. Any reproduction of this book by any means without express permission from the publisher will be deemed a breach of copyright. Any reviewer of this book may use short excerpts of this book without previous permission.

Copyright © 2019
Lloyd English

ISBN 978 1979921701

My Guitar Pal Series

Theory, Practice, Understanding

The **My Guitar Pal Series** of method books is a unique approach to method books and guitar instruction. Each book is presented in a logical and progressive manner that is designed to lead the student toward a greater practical understanding of the instrument and a deeper understanding of music language generally.

The purpose of this book is not to relate a lot of theoretical information but instead to build a solid and ever increasing practical understanding that will provide you with the tools to make music. This approach is expressed by presenting each page as a new lesson with clear instruction and application to the fretboard.

For the guitar instructor this book can add a new dimension to any comprehensive teaching program and will without doubt enhance the educational experience. This entire series has been proved through many thousands of private lessons before going to print and will thus save you many hours of preparation time while providing the best result for your students.

Online video lessons that support material in the series is available at www.MyGuitarPal.com.

We hope that this book and others in the series will lead you to ever greater musical adventures.

Copyright 2018 by My Pal Online Education Inc.

My GuitarPal
www.myguitarpal.com

All rights reserved. No part of this book may be reproduced in any form or by any means now known or known in the future, including all information storage and retrieval systems without express permission in writing from the publisher except by reviewers who may quote brief passages for the purpose of review only.

TABLE OF CONTENTS

Table of Contents 3
Introduction 4
How To Practice 5
How To Use This Book 6

SECTION 1
Theory & Harmony Fundamentals
Natural Notes on the Fretboard 8
What Is An Arpeggio? 9
Chord Progressions Numbering & Function . 10
Major & Minor Triads 11
Chord Spellings 12
Spelling Intervals and Chords 13
Spelling Major, Minor, Diminished, Aug . 14

SECTION 2
Fretboard Application
Major 7 16
C Major 7, Root 6, 5, 2 17
Progressions For Practice 18
Dominant 7 19
G7 (Dom7) Root 6, 5, 2 20
Progressions For Practice 21
More Progressions For Practice 22
Minor 7 23
D Minor 7 Root 6, 5, 2 24
Progressions For Practice 25

SECTION 3
Understanding Relative & Parallel Harmony
Introduction to the Minor Key 27
Parallel and Relative 28
C Minor 7 29
C Minor 7 Root 6, 5, 2 30
II Chords in a Minor Key 31
D Minor 7b5 32
D Minor 7b5 Root 6, 5, 2 33
Progressions For Practice 34
Harmonic Minor Scale & 7b9 Chord . . . 35
7b9 Arpeggio 36
G7b9 Root 6, 5, 2 37
Progressions For Practice 38

Harmonic, Melodic & Jazz Minor Scales 39
Composite Harmony 40
Composite Progressions 41
Night And Day Harmonic Analysis 42

SECTION 4
Tension Leading Toward Resolution
Diminished 7 Chord 44
Diminished 7 Arpeggio 45
Progressions For Practice 46
Altered Dominant Sounds 47
G7#5 or Augmented 7 48
G7b5 Root 6, 5, 2 49
G7#9 Root 6, 5, 2 50

SECTION 5
Root on Strings 3 & 4, Chords & Arpeggios
The CAGED System 52
CAGED System from C 53
Voice Leading 54
Root 4 and 3 Forms 55
Major 7 Root 4, 3 56
Dominant 7 Root 4, 3 57
Minor 7 Root 4, 3 58
Minor 7b5 Root 4, 3 59
Connecting The Fretboard 60
CAGED Connections (Major Scale) . . . 61
CAGED Connections (Mixolydian) 62
CAGED Connections (Natural Minor) . . 63
Spelling Intervals & Chords 64
Chord Voicing Glossary
    Major 66
    Dominant 68
    Minor 71
    Diminished (Dominant) 73
Enharmonic Equivalents 74
Short History of the Rhythm Chord 75
Short History of the Real Fake Book . . . 76
Master Fretboard 77
Glossary of Terms 78

Essentials for the Improvising Guitarist

This book is ideal for the developing guitarist wishing to acquire a grasp of the linear or melodic expression of chord sounds. The material presented here applies to every player wishing to improvise and expand their understanding.

The serious student will develop a conceptual working knowledge of common sounds and fingerings that are functional from a musical and technical perspective.

Think of the arpeggio as a moveable melodic representation of a chord that doesn't lock your hand into chordal forms but instead allows for individual note choices that express harmonies. This approach to a linear expression of chord voicings will lead to defining the harmony of the chosen song material and will provide countless harmonic, melodic and creative variations, no matter what the style.

Remember that learning new sounds requires building an understanding of how they are used idiomatically. Notes work when they sound right in musical context - be sensitive to the "stylistic" potential of what you are learning. Develop your own phrases, inventions and ideas while using arpeggio forms as sonic templates for the development of horizontal line informed by chordal thinking.

Improvisation is about deconstructing and reconstructing. Stick to the basic concepts of "chords come from scales" and "arpeggios come from chords" and organize those sonic ideas on the fretboard.

Play-along tracks and additional materials are available at www.myguitarpal.com.

HOW TO PRACTICE

Perfect Practice Makes Perfect

Practising requires as much physical work as it does mental work and this holds especially true for the Guitar. If your practising is rushed or unfocused your time will be largely wasted and your progress will be negatively impacted. With this in mind use your time wisely and carefully, be patient and observe the following.

1. Build a private and quiet practice place that includes all the items you will need including a music stand, guitar stand, picks, pencils, music you are working on, a tuner and a small table. This should be a place you want to go to and should have all the elements required for a productive session.

2. Begin by establishing a Timeframe for your practice session and then divide that Timeframe into smaller tasks . Create a group of tasks to achieve and then apply the time frames to the tasks.

   Example: 30 minutes divided

Scales	– 10 minutes
Repertoire	– 10 minutes
Triads	– 10 minutes

3. Play and practice at a tempo at which you are making no mistakes, never play faster than you can think, always "slowly and accurately".

4. Repetitions of the task should always be with full concentration with your ears wide open, listen for a musical result.

5. If you get bored redirect your attention. Work with steady concentration and stay focused, clear your mind and concentrate.

6. Make sure your instrument is always tuned perfectly, use a digital tuner. The sounds that are coming from your instrument should make you excited to practice. Never be satisfied with anything less than an enjoyable musical experience.

For more ideas on practice go to the My Guitar Pal blog at http://myguitarpal.com/blog/

HOW TO USE THIS BOOK

Every arpeggio type is first explained by how it is derived from its parent scale. For example a C major 7 arpeggio is explained as the I chord in the key of C major and the notes for that arpeggio are derived from the 1, 3, 5 and 7 degrees of that scale.

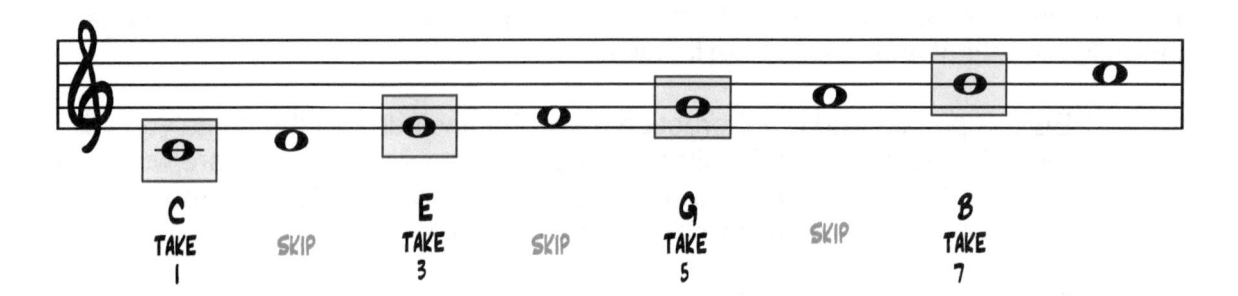

Arpeggio and Chord Diagrams:

The circled numbers in the Arpeggio and Chord diagrams represent the Scale Degree (large numbers) and Fingerings (small numbers). Number 1 in the black circle is the Root or naming note.

Roman Numeral in this case designates hand position or where finger 1 is placed.

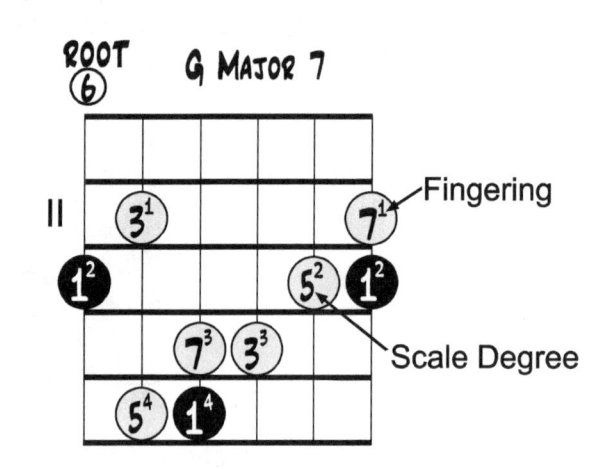

Progressions For Practice:

At the end of each arpeggio section there are suggested progressions for practice. These progressions should be used for practice while following the circled root designations suggested. Begin by practicing the arpeggio forms from their given root.

Example:

Each of the play-along progressions can be found at www.MyGuitarPal.com

Section 1

THEORY & HARMONY FUNDAMENTALS

Understanding the fundamental elements of harmony as expressed on the guitar fretboard

NATURAL NOTES ON THE FRETBOARD
Chord & Arpeggio Roots

Here are the names of the natural notes on the guitar fretboard for the purpose of identifying chord and arpeggio roots and names associated with the chord forms being studied.

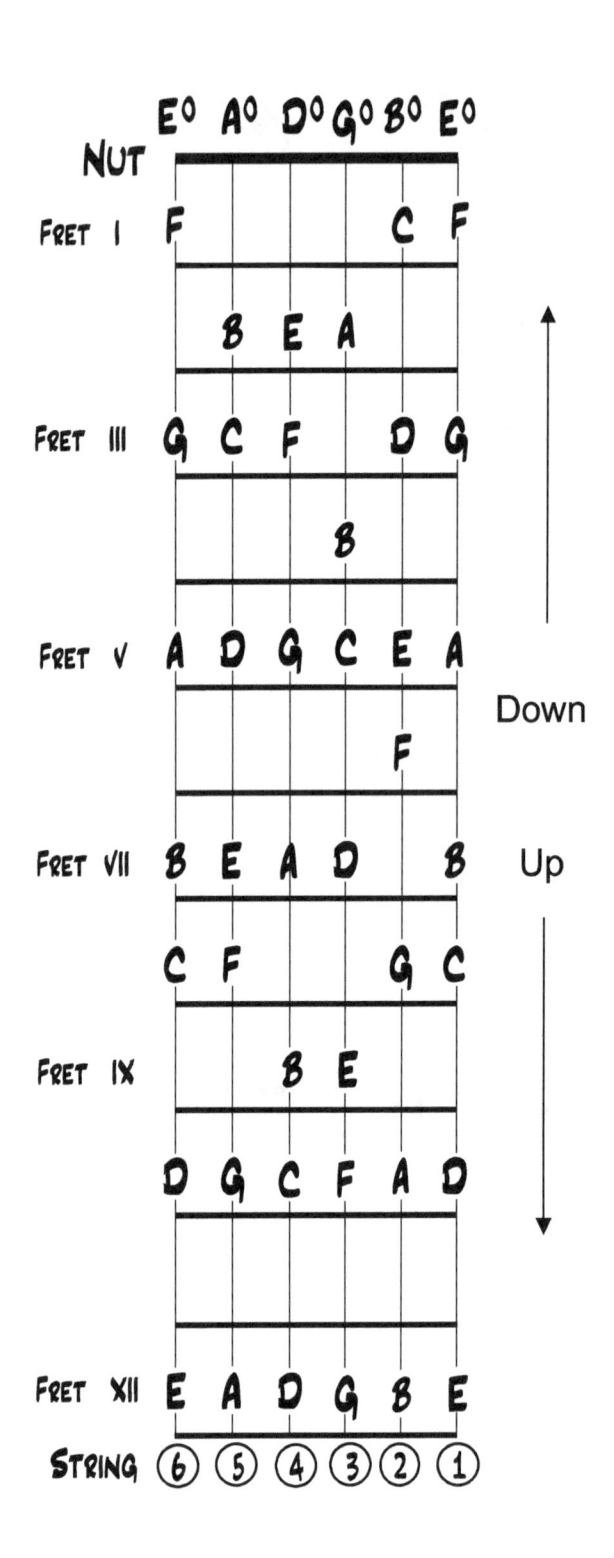

Sharps & Flats

- Between B & C, and E & F there are no sharps or flats.

- Moving any natural note a semitone toward the headstock lowers the note.

- When lowered a semitone:
    A-A♭ G-G♭ F-E E-E♭
    D-D♭ C-B B-B♭

- Moving any natural note 1 fret toward the body will raise the note a semitone.

- When raised a semitone:
    A-A# B-C C-C# D-D#
    E-F F-F# G-G#

- Notes with the same pitch but a different name are called enharmonic, as:
    A#/B♭ or C#/D♭

- Natural notes correspond to the white keys on the piano.

WHAT IS AN ARPEGGIO

Chords and arpeggios are derived from scales. When we build a chord we use Tertian harmony or harmony constructed in thirds. The notes in a chord are heard simultaneously, and the notes in an arpeggio are heard separately or melodically.

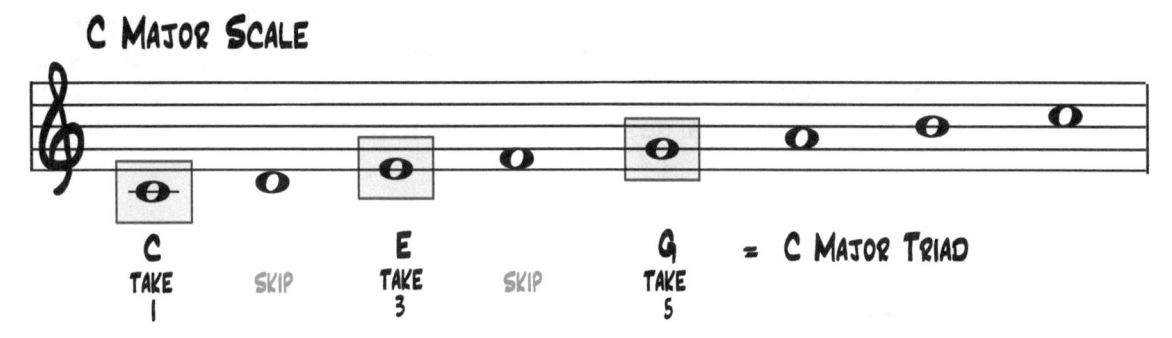

C Major Scale

C - TAKE 1, SKIP, E - TAKE 3, SKIP, G - TAKE 5 = C Major Triad

This will produce a triad or 3-note chord. We call these notes the 1, 3 and 5 of the chord no matter what degree of the scale we start from. If we extend this logic to a 7th chord type we move one third further as:

TAKE 1 — SKIP — TAKE 3 — SKIP — TAKE 5 — SKIP — TAKE 7 (3rd, 3rd, 3rd)

The chord derived in the example below is a major 7th chord which is a 4-note chord. For example, a C Major 7 chord can be 1- 3 - 5 - 7 of a C major scale:

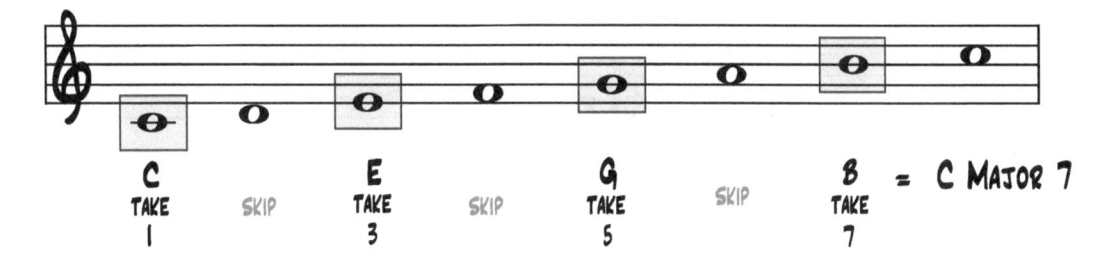

C - TAKE 1, SKIP, E - TAKE 3, SKIP, G - TAKE 5, SKIP, B - TAKE 7 = C Major 7

Major 7 Arpeggio

II Position

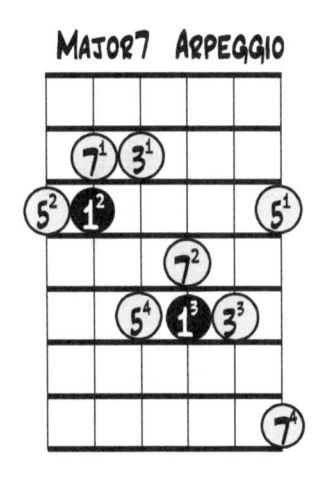

On the guitar fretboard the notes **C E G B** when spread over II position would appear in a vertical arpeggio form as in the diagram on the left.

NOTE: Roman numerals are often used to designate scale degrees. For the sake of space in this book we are using corresponding Arabic large numbers for scale degrees, Roman Numerals are used for hand position and small numbers for fingering.

I	II	III		HAND POSITION
1	3	5	7	SCALE DEGREES
1	2	3	4	FINGERING

CHORD PROGRESSION
Numbering and Function

Every Arpeggio is derived from degrees of a scale. As previously mentioned, the I chord is derived in thirds from degree I of the major scale. When counted to the VII degree in a C major scale it is a CMaj7, a four-note chord. A Roman Numeral refers to the "degree" of the scale from which the chord derives its letter name or root, as I chord or II chord or V chord, etc. In this case, this Roman numeral designation refers to chord function, not a fretboard position.

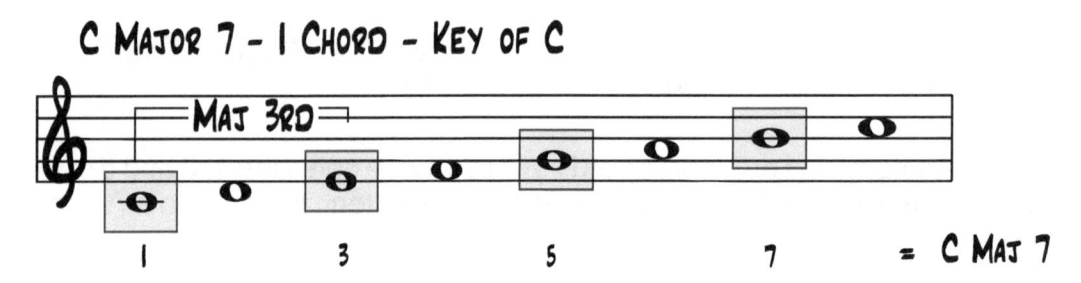

C Major 7 - I Chord - Key of C

The II chord begins on the second degree of the Major scale. The root of the chord is D or 1, the 3rd is F, 5th is A and the 7th is C. The distance from the D to the F is a minor 3rd thus making the chord minor (to be covered in detail later).

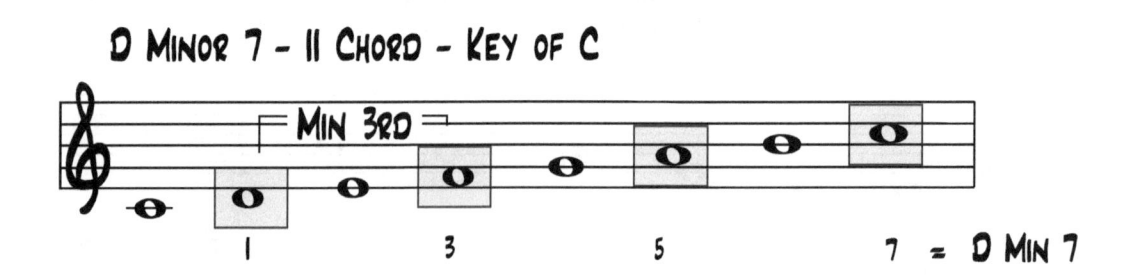

D Minor 7 - II Chord - Key of C

The V or V7 chord is derived from the V or dominant degree of the major scale. For this reason the chord is referred to as the dominant or dominant 7.

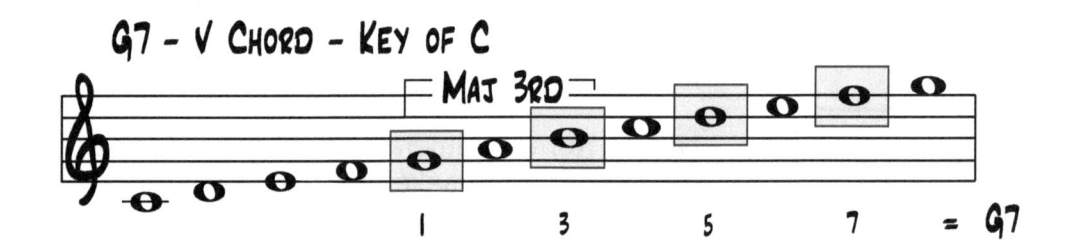

G7 - V Chord - Key of C

Each of the above chords of C Maj 7, Dmin7 and G7 have different functions, different spellings and different sounds.

MAJOR & MINOR TRIADS

A major third interval is the distance of 2 tones.

Ex.

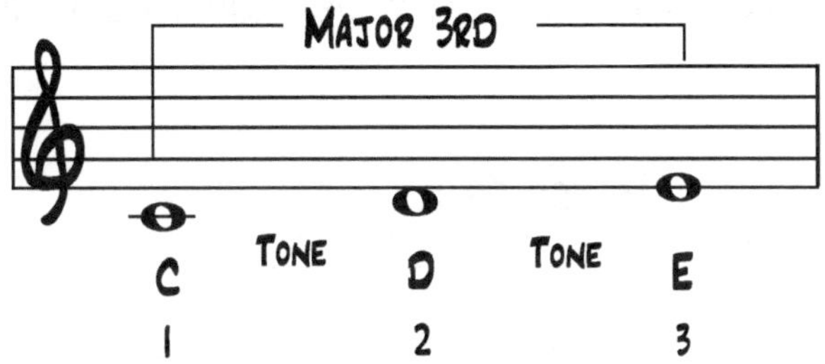

2 whole steps

c d e
w w

A minor third interval is the distance of 1 tone plus 1 semitone.

Ex.

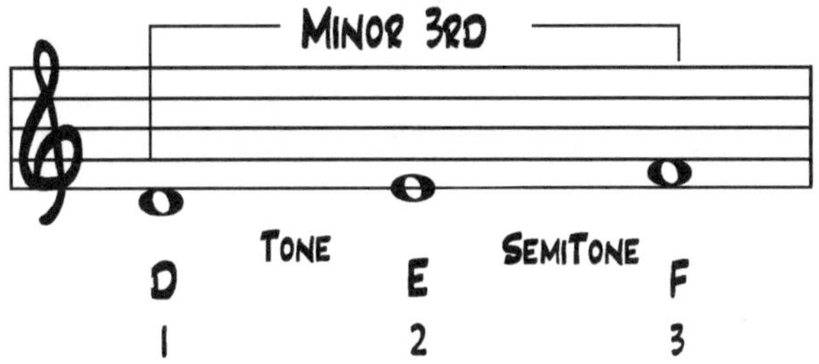

1 whole step + 1 half-step

c d e f
w w h

A major triad begins with a major 3rd.

Ex.

C MAJOR

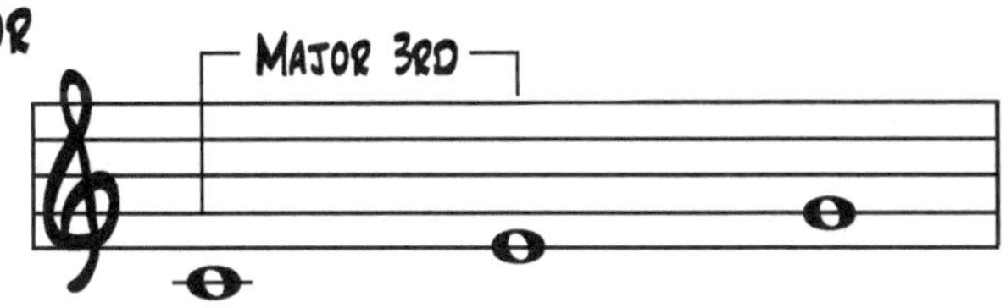

major 3rd
c d e
w w
2 whole steps

A minor triad begins with a minor 3rd.

Ex.

D MINOR

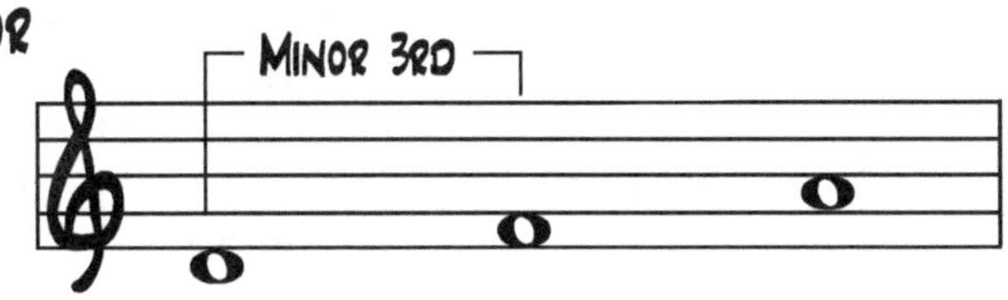

minor 3rd
c d e f
w w h

CHORD SPELLINGS

A 4-note chord counted in thirds from its root is called a 7 chord, 1, 3, 5, 7. The three different 7 chord types to be covered in the first portion of this book are Major 7, minor 7 and Dominant 7. Think of each of these chords as a triad with either a major or minor 7th interval from the root. A minor 7th interval is a semitone smaller than a major 7th.

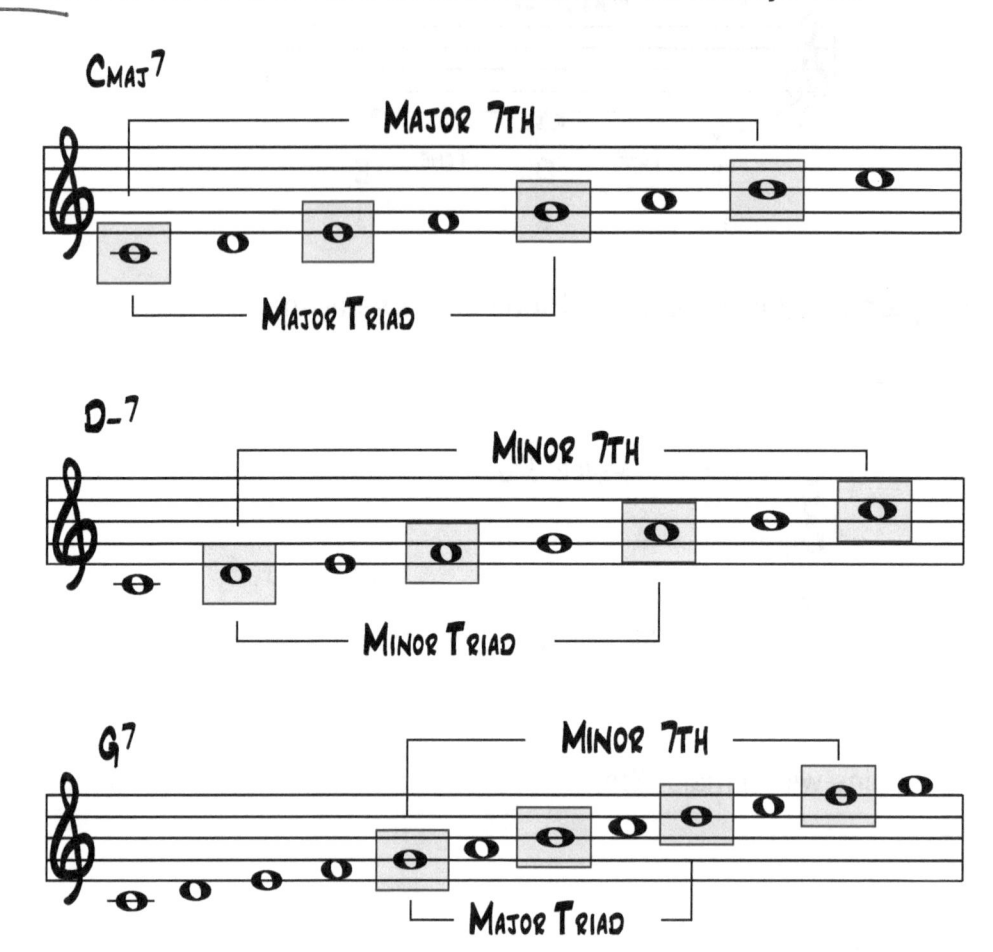

Within the context of this study it is helpful to understand each of these chord types as serving a different harmonic function within a key. These functions are broadly defined by varying degrees of tension. A state of resolution has no tension.

Common Chord Function Within a Key

I Chord	Major 7	Tonic	No tension	Resolution
II Chord	Minor 7	Subdominant	Medium tension	Leads to Tonic or Dominant
V Chord	7	Dominant	High tension	Leads to Tonic

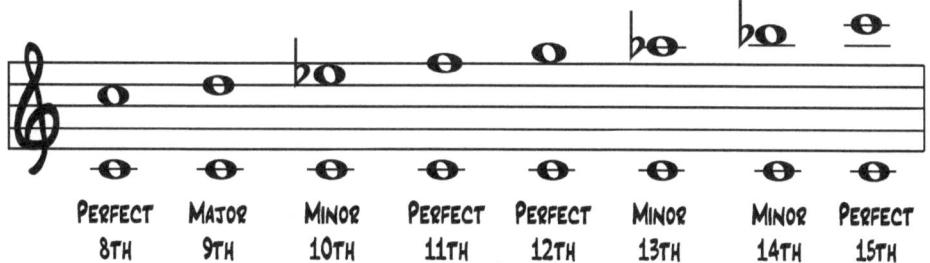

SPELLING INTERVALS AND CHORDS

An interval is the distance between two notes. Let's begin by naming the interval distances in the major scale from the root or tonic.

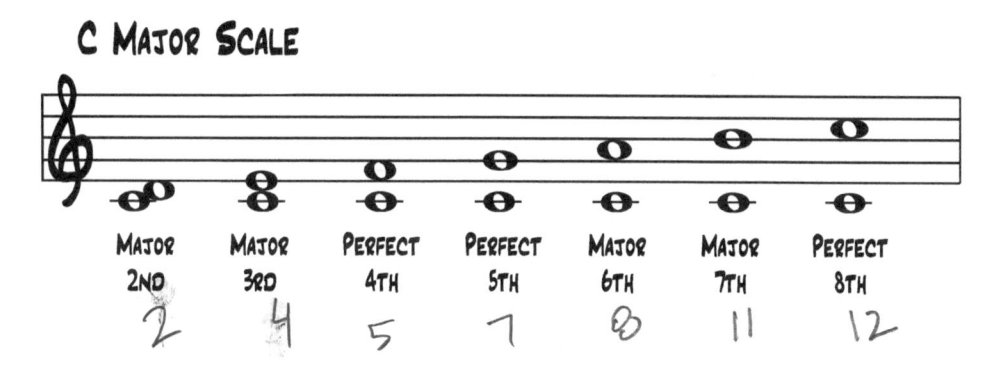

C Major Scale

Major 2nd	Major 3rd	Perfect 4th	Perfect 5th	Major 6th	Major 7th	Perfect 8th
2	4	5	7	8	11	12

Compound intervals go past the octave as:

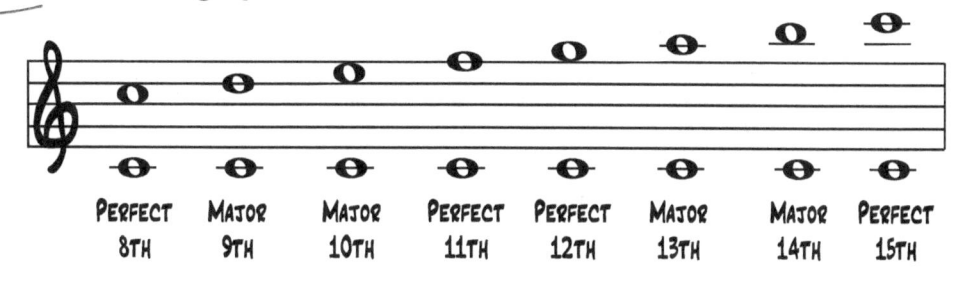

Perfect 8th, Major 9th, Major 10th, Perfect 11th, Perfect 12th, Major 13th, Major 14th, Perfect 15th

C Natural Minor Scale

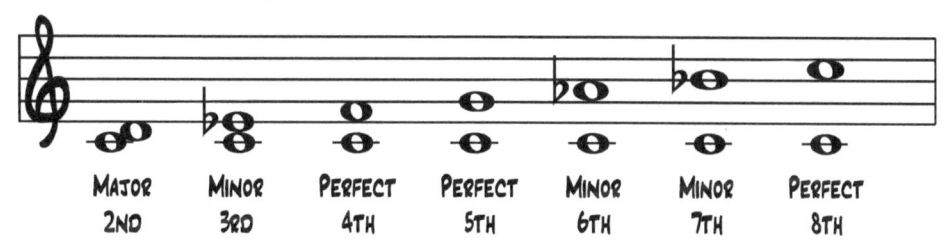

Major 2nd, Minor 3rd, Perfect 4th, Perfect 5th, Minor 6th, Minor 7th, Perfect 8th

Compound intervals

Perfect 8th, Major 9th, Minor 10th, Perfect 11th, Perfect 12th, Minor 13th, Minor 14th, Perfect 15th

SPELLING INTERVALS AND CHORDS

Major, Minor, Diminished, Augmented

The distance of the 3rd from the root of the chord will define whether a chord is major or minor. The distance of a major 3rd is two tones.

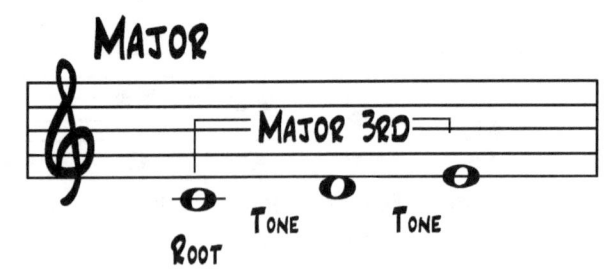

The distance of a minor 3rd is a tone plus a semitone.
A tone is a distance of two frets, a semitone is the distance of one fret.

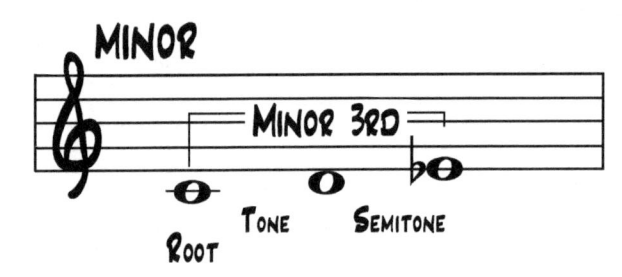

When building chords from the root note by stacking 3rds we can create the following four triadic chordal building blocks:

Major Triad	Major 3rd plus minor 3rd
Minor Triad	Minor 3rd plus Major 3rd
Diminished Triad	Minor 3rd plus minor 3rd
Augmented Triad	Major 3rd plus Major 3rd

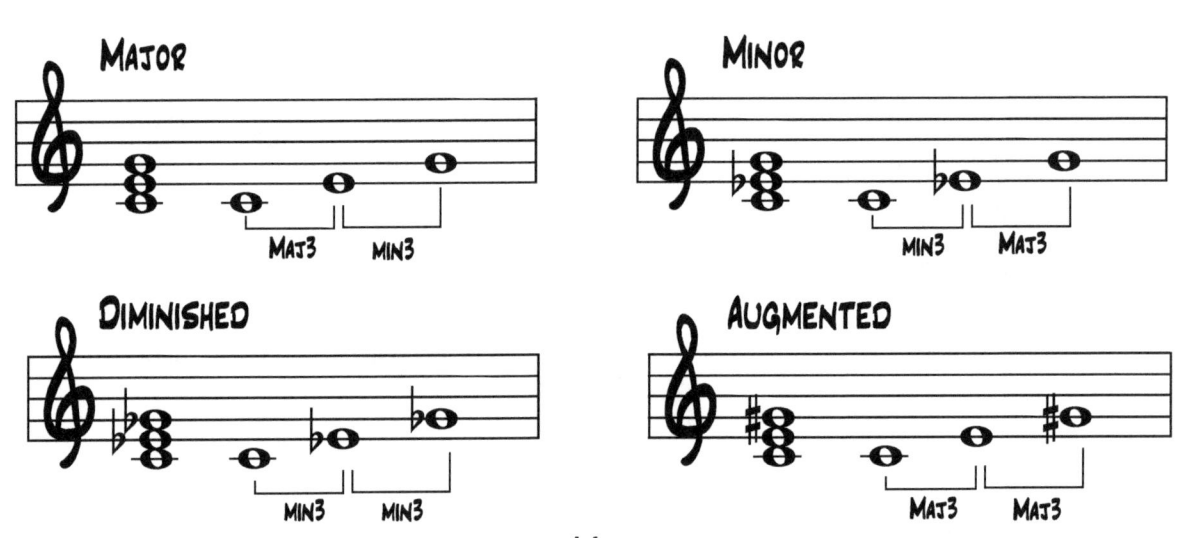

Section 2

FRETBOARD APPLICATION

Chord and arpeggio forms as applied to the fretboard

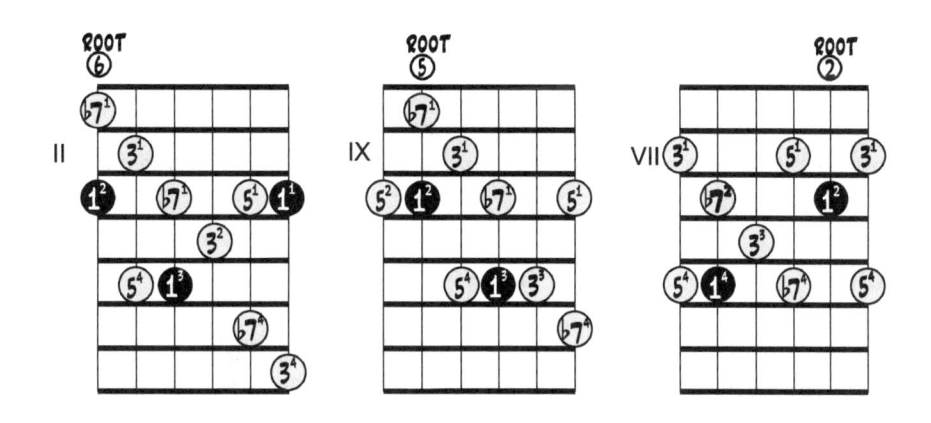

MAJOR 7

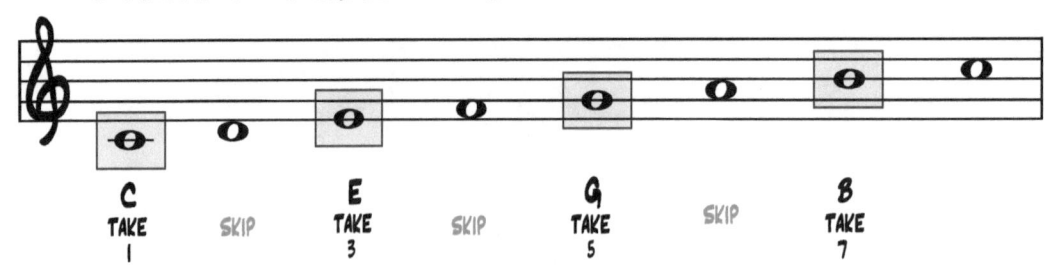

C Major 7 - I Chord - Tonic - Key of C

C TAKE 1 — SKIP — E TAKE 3 — SKIP — G TAKE 5 — SKIP — B TAKE 7

Each arpeggio fingering diagram will repeat the notes as they would appear in the related scale and until all possible notes are played within that vertical position (without shifts).

Note that the Major 7 arpeggio is spelled with a major 3rd from the root and a major 7th interval from the root.

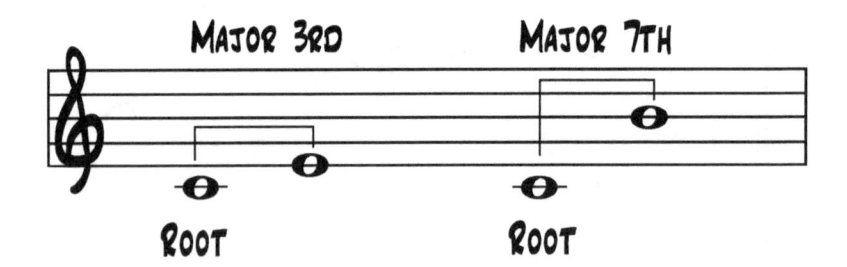

Major 3rd — Major 7th
Root — Root

Be sure to execute and practice each arpeggio form with identical fingering ascending and descending. Practice slowly and carefully.

Once you begin to feel comfortable with the arpeggio forms then begin to associate them with their related chord forms. Always be aware of the location of the root or naming note of each chord and arpeggio.

REPETITION

To be clearer on the topic of repetition, strive for absolutely clean repetitions with no mistakes. As for number of reps - for a simple form I would suggest 10 to begin with and eventually work to 30 to 50. This *will* provide results, and once you get into the habit the time will pass quickly.

C MAJOR 7
ROOT 6, 5, 2

ARPEGGIO

e shape (Root 6)
a shape (Root 5)
C shape (Root 2)

CHORD

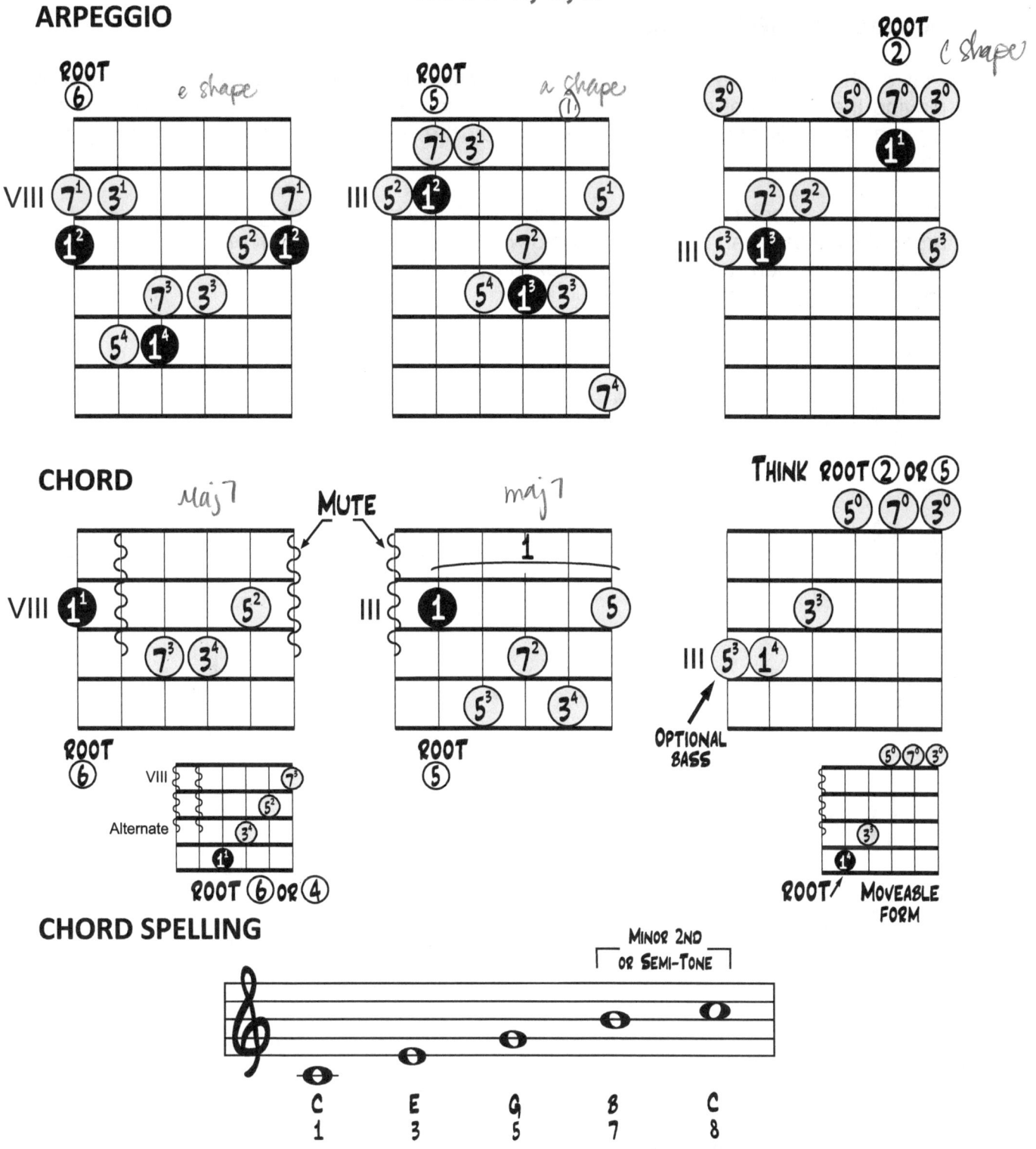

Maj7 (Root 6)
MUTE
maj7 (Root 5)
Think Root 2 or 5

Optional Bass

Root 6 Alternate — Root 6 or 4

Root / Moveable Form

CHORD SPELLING

Minor 2nd or Semi-Tone

C - E - G - B - C
1 - 3 - 5 - 7 - 8

NOTE: All arpeggio forms are moveable but are shown as Cmaj7 in the above diagrams. Practice any forms in open position as moveable forms as well. Make sure to follow the fingerings carefully, identically ascending and descending.

PROGRESSIONS FOR PRACTICE

How to Use the Written Progressions

Play each of these progressions for chord practice as well as arpeggio practice. Start by playing the chords at a relaxed tempo and once comfortable with that move on to the arpeggios slowly and carefully. Always play the fingerings identically ascending and descending.

Start your practice at a slow tempo and eventually try to avoid going back to the root of the arpeggio, instead start the next arpeggio where the last one has left off. Therefore, if you are on string 2 then stay there for the next arpeggio form as well, thereby "voice leading" to the next arpeggio form or chord.

EXERCISE

1. 4/4 ‖: Cmaj7 / / / | D♭maj7 / / / | Dmaj7 / / / | D♭maj7 / / / :‖
   *⑤   ⑤   ⑤   ⑤

2. 4/4 ‖: Dmaj7 / / / | E♭maj7 / / / | Dmaj7 / / / | E♭maj7 / / / :‖
   ⑤   ⑤   ⑤   ⑤

3. 4/4 ‖: Gmaj7 / / / | A♭maj7 / / / | Gmaj7 / / / | A♭maj7 / / / :‖
   ⑥   ⑥   ⑥   ⑥

4. 4/4 ‖: Amaj7 / / / | B♭maj7 / / / | Amaj7 / / / | B♭maj7 / / / :‖
   ⑥   ⑥   ⑥   ⑥

5. 4/4 ‖: Cmaj7 / / / | E♭maj7 / / / | A♭maj7 / / / | Cmaj7 / / / :‖
   ⑤   ②   ⑥   ⑤

6. 4/4 ‖: Amaj7 / / / | Fmaj7 / / / | B♭maj7 / / / | Amaj7 / / / :‖
   ⑥   ⑤ ②   ⑥   ⑥

✱ Note that the circled numbers are chord and arpeggio roots.

Play-Along Tracks at www.MyGuitarPal.com

DOMINANT 7

The Dominant 7 chord is built from the V degree or Dominant note of a Major scale.

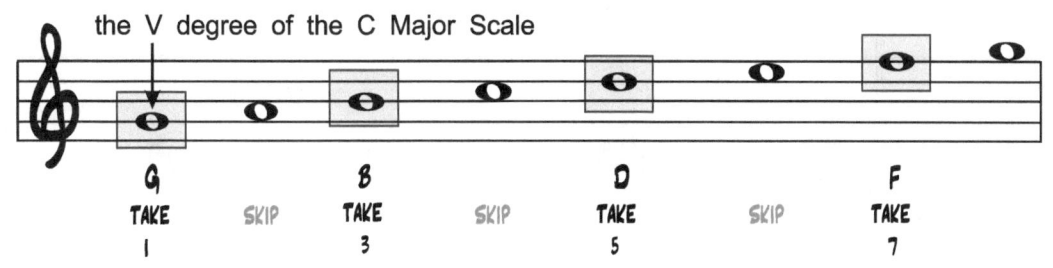

The dominant 7th chord is not to be confused with the Major 7 chord. Not only do they have different functions but different spellings and sounds as well. Let's examine the spellings of the two chords (arpeggios) from the same root.

The dominant 7 chord has a minor 7th distance from the root of the chord and the major 7 chord has a major 7th distance from the root. When examining their structure from the same root or in "parallel" (same root) the difference in spelling is apparent.

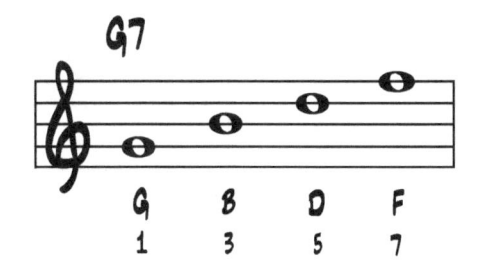

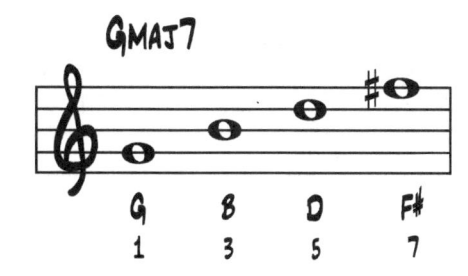

Note that both chords are a major triad with a different 7th. The dominant 7th chord is a minor 7th interval from the root while the major 7th is a major 7th interval from the root. There is a semitone difference between the two.

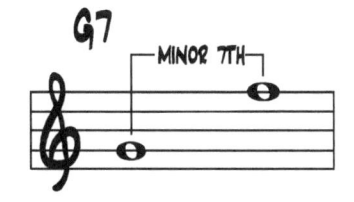

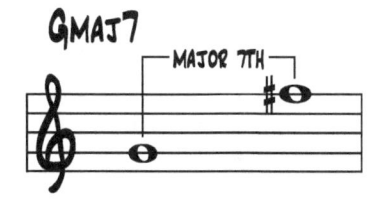

If we were to move from a Gmaj7 chord to a G7 chord only one note would change, the F♯ would fall to an F natural. In order to differentiate a Major 7 chord from a 7 chord we call the 7th of a dominant 7th chord a flat (♭7). Note this designation within the arpeggio forms.

19

G7
(Dominant 7)
ROOT 6, 5, 2

ARPEGGIO

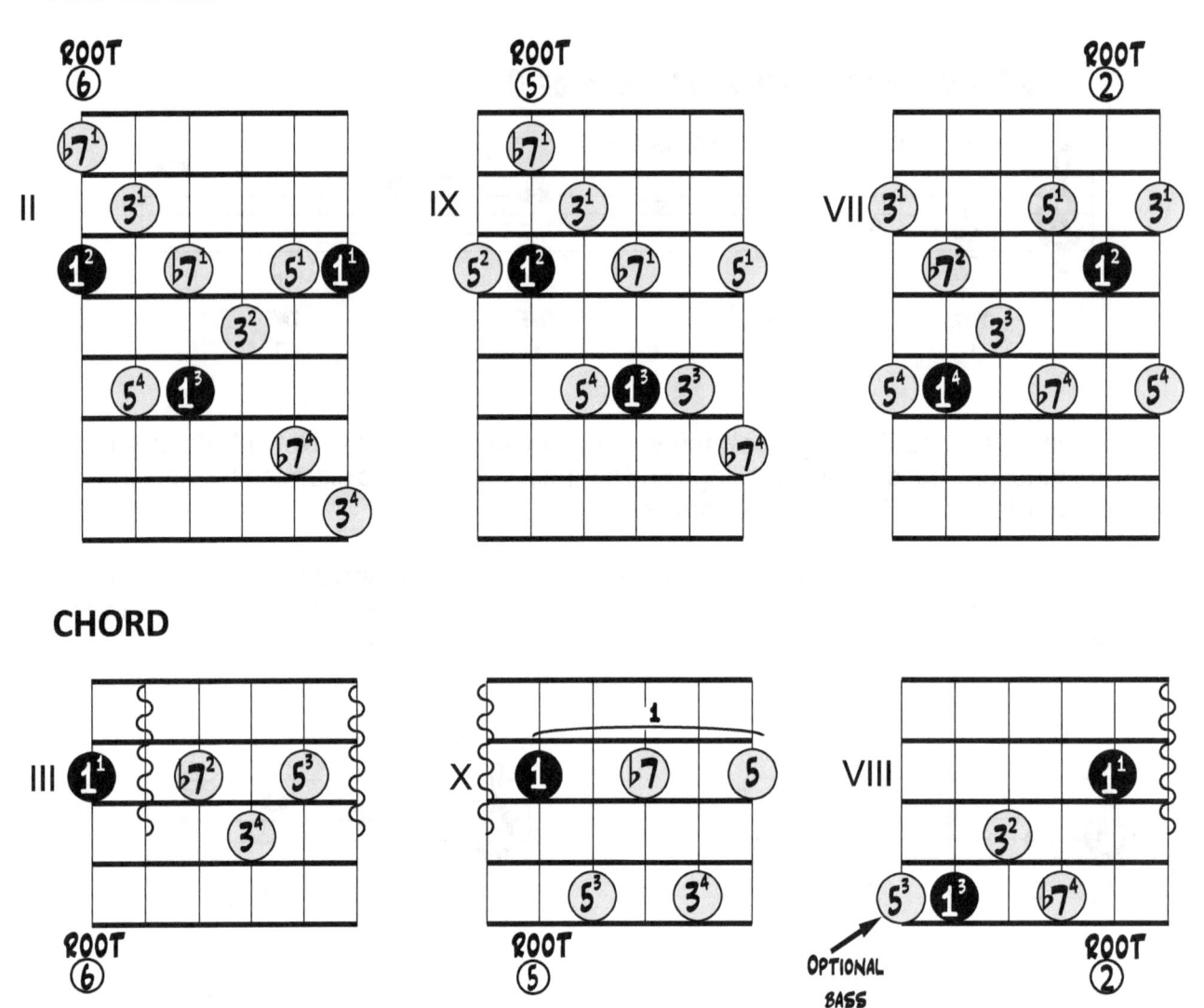

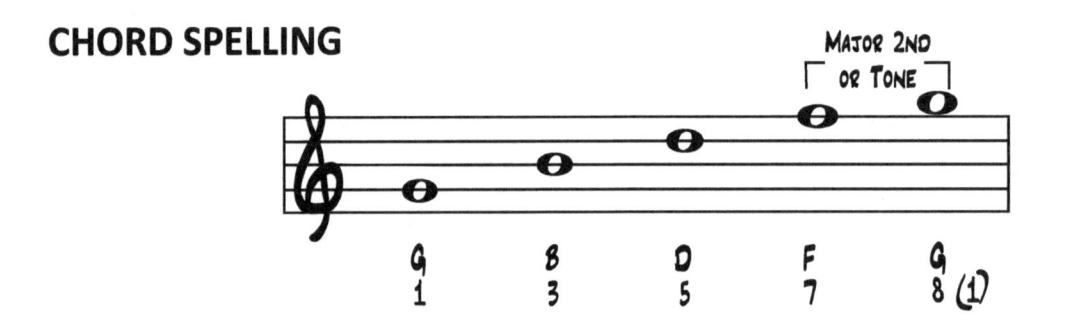

CHORD

CHORD SPELLING

G   B   D   F   G
1   3   5   7   8 (1)

NOTE: All arpeggio forms are moveable but are shown as G7 above. Try moving them around the fretboard. Roman numerals designate fretboard position for G7.

PROGRESSIONS FOR PRACTICE

The following progressions for practice are V to I progressions in eight different keys. The circled roots indicated are not the only way to play each of these progressions but are provided as a practical starting point. Try resolving to the 1 chord from every string.

EXERCISE

1. 4/4 ‖: G7 / / / | ％ | Cmaj7 / / / | ％ :‖
   ⑥   ⑤

2. 4/4 ‖: D7 / / / | ％ | Gmaj7 / / / | ％ :‖
   ⑤   ⑥

3. 4/4 ‖: E7 / / / | ％ | Amaj7 / / / | ％ :‖
   ②   ⑥

4. 4/4 ‖: A7 / / / | ％ | Dmaj7 / / / | ％ :‖
   ⑥   ②

5. 4/4 ‖: F#7 / / / | ％ | Bmaj7 / / / | ％ :‖
   ⑥   ⑤

6. 4/4 ‖: Eb7 / / / | ％ | Abmaj7 / / / | ％ :‖
   ②   ⑥

7. 4/4 ‖: F7 / / / | ％ | Bbmaj7 / / / | ％ :‖
   ②   ⑥

8. 4/4 ‖: B7 / / / | ％ | Emaj7 / / / | ％ :‖
   ⑥   ⑤

The progressions on the following page use only dominant 7 chords. There are three basic 12-bar blues progressions used as well as a cycle of dominants. The cycle is particularly challenging so it would be a good idea to begin by taking it in segments adding one new chord at a time to the progression.

Play-along tracks are available at **www.MyGuitarPal.com**.

MORE PROGRESSIONS FOR PRACTICE

Note the indicated chord roots below the chord names.

BLUES IN G

G^7 / / /	C^7 / / /	G^7 / / /	⁒
⑥	⑤	⑥	
C^7 / / /	⁒	G^7 / / /	⁒
⑤		⑥	
D^7 / / /	C^7 / / /	G^7 / / /	D^7 / / /
②	⑤	⑥	②

BLUES IN C

C^7 / / /	F^7 / / /	C^7 / / /	⁒
⑤	②	⑤	
F^7 / / /	⁒	C^7 / / /	⁒
⑥		②	
G^7 / / /	F^7 / / /	C^7 / / /	G^7 / / /
⑥	⑥	⑥	⑥

BLUES IN B♭

$B^{♭7}$ / / /	⁒	⁒	⁒
⑥			
$E^{♭7}$ / / /	⁒	$B^{♭7}$ / / /	⁒
②		⑥	
F^7 / / /	$B^{♭7}$ / / /	$E^{♭7}$ / / /	F^7 / / /
②	⑥	⑤	②

THE CYCLE OF DOMINANTS

C^7 / / /	F^7 / / /	$B^{♭7}$ / / /	$E^{♭7}$ / / /
⑥	⑤	⑥	⑤
$A^{♭7}$ / / /	$D^{♭7}$ / / /	$G^{♭7}$ / / /	B^7 / / /
⑥	⑤	⑥	⑤
E^7 / / /	A^7 / / /	D^7 / / /	G^7 / / /
②	⑥	②	⑥

There are several different ways to play each of these progressions with the chords and arpeggios covered thus far, so try as many combinations as possible in your practice.

minor 7

The minor 7 chord can be built from the II degree of a Major scale.

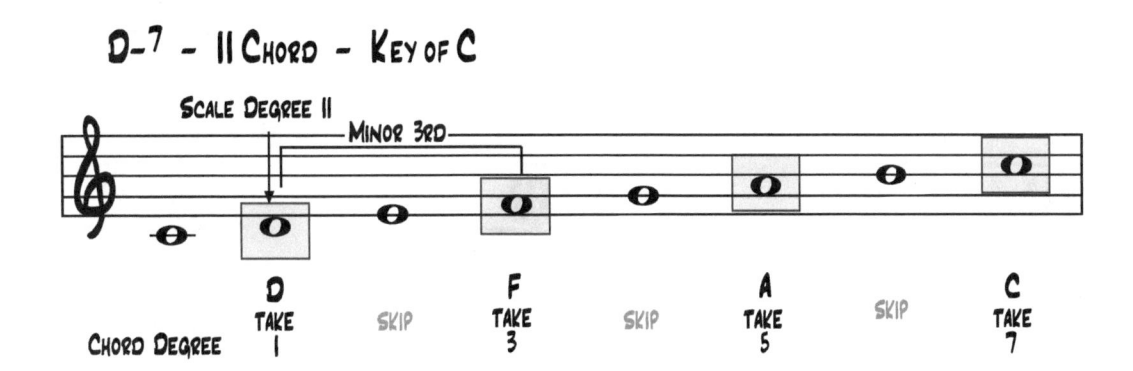

D-7 - II Chord - Key of C

The notes of a Dm7 chord are: D F A C. Note that the distance between the D and F, or the 1st and 3rd of the chord is a minor 3rd, a tone plus a semi-tone. The sound of "minor" is in the minor 3rd distance between 1 and 3 whether it be a scale, chord or arpeggio.

When we examine the arpeggios in "parallel" or from *the same root,* the differences in each of their spellings becomes clear.

IN PARALLEL (SAME ROOT)

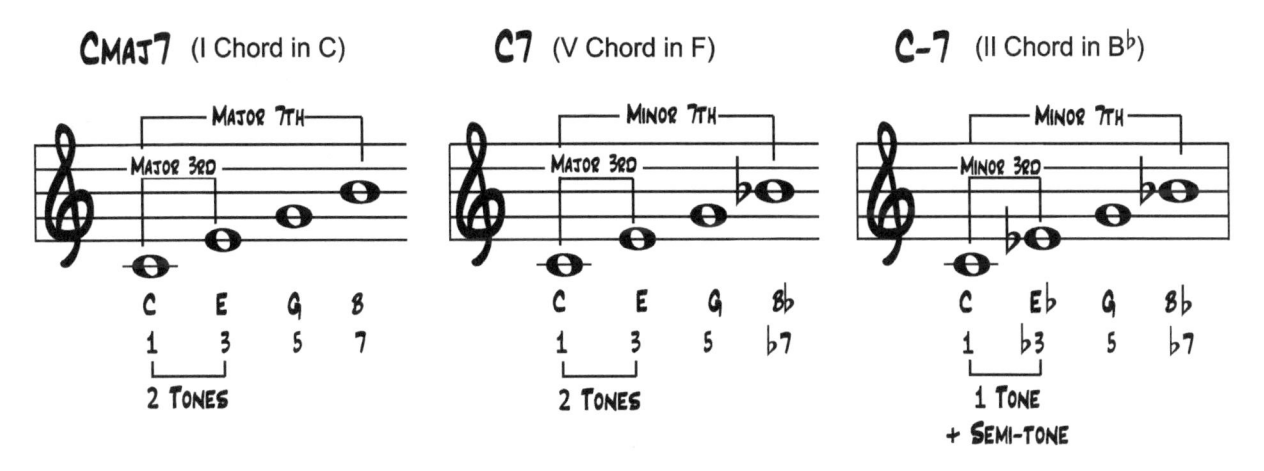

CMAJ7 (I Chord in C) — C7 (V Chord in F) — C-7 (II Chord in B♭)

Chord Type	Intervals from Root
Major 7	Maj 3, Maj 7
7	Maj 3, min 7
minor 7	min 3, min 7

D minor 7
ROOT 6, 5, 2

ARPEGGIO

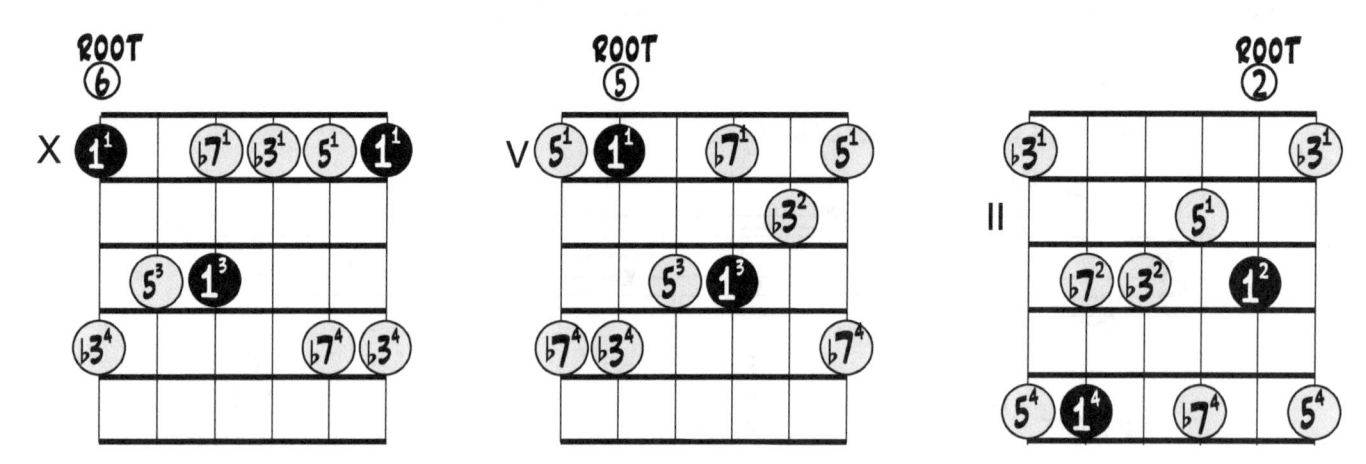

Note that even though the root is present on more than one string, the indicated root is there for practical purposes that will become apparent.

CHORD

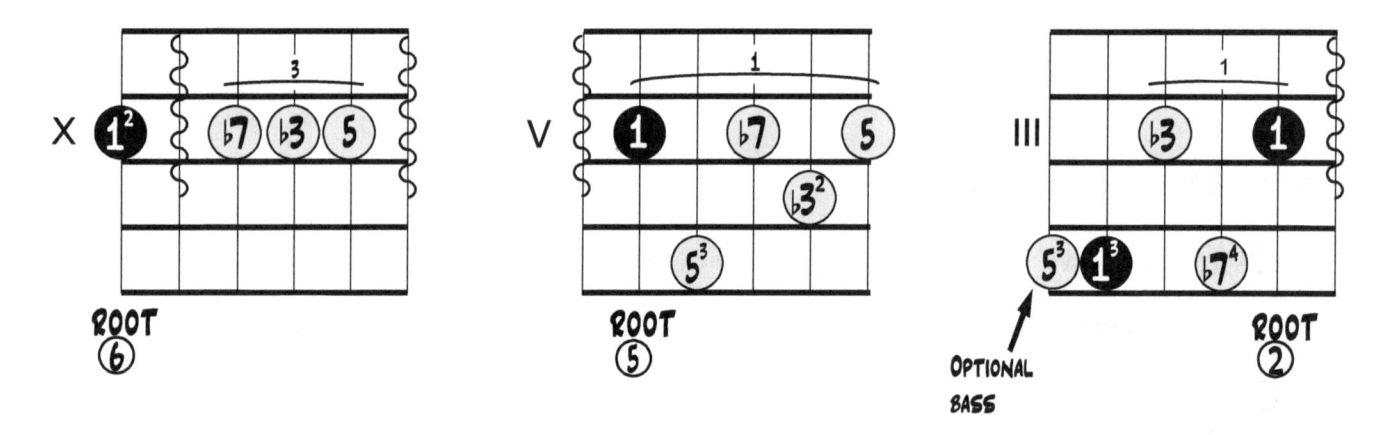

CHORD SPELLING

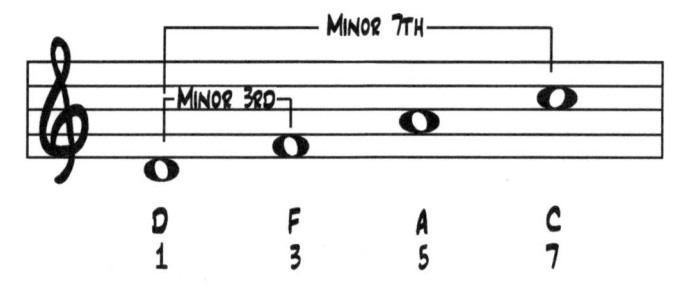

D	F	A	C
1	3	5	7

Minor 3rd: D to F
Minor 7th: D to C

NOTE: All arpeggio forms are moveable but are shown in the above diagrams as Dmin7 or the II chord in the key of C. ♭7 is a minor 7th from the root. ♭3 is a minor 3rd from the root.

PROGRESSIONS FOR PRACTICE

The chords examined thus far have each been built from a degree of the major scale. The major 7 from degree I, the 7 from degree V and the minor 7 from degree II.

The following progressions are called II V I progressions because they use the chords built on those degrees of the scale. Use them for practice and memorize them.

Make sure to use the string roots suggested to start.

Exercise	II	V	I		Key
1	D-7 ⑤	G7 ⑥	Cmaj7 ⑤	%	C
2	A-7 ⑥	D7 ②	Gmaj7 ⑥	%	G
3	E-7 ②	A7 ⑥	Dmaj7 ②	%	D
4	B-7 ⑥	E7 ⑤	Amaj7 ⑥	%	A
5	F#-7 ⑤	B7 ⑥	Emaj7 ②	%	E
6	C#-7 ⑤	F#7 ②	Bmaj7 ⑤	%	B
7	Ab-7 ⑥	Db7 ⑤	Gbmaj7 ⑥	%	Gb
8	Eb-7 ②	Ab7 ⑥	Dbmaj7 ⑤	%	Db
9	Bb-7 ⑥	Eb7 ⑤	Abmaj7 ⑥	%	Ab
10	F-7 ②	Bb7 ⑥	Ebmaj7 ②	%	Eb
11	C-7 ⑥	F7 ⑤	Bbmaj7 ⑥	%	Bb
12	G-7 ②	C7 ⑥	Fmaj7 ⑤	%	F

All exercises are in 4/4 time with repeat signs.

Play-along tracks are available at **www.MyGuitarPal.com**.

Section 3

UNDERSTANDING RELATIVE AND PARALLEL HARMONY

A practical examination of the most characteristic use of harmony and chord progression

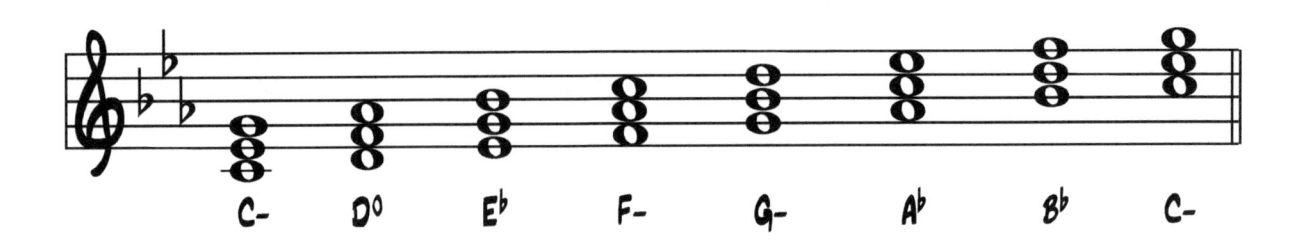

C− D° E♭ F− G− A♭ B♭ C−

INTRODUCTION TO THE MINOR KEY

Chords and arpeggios are derived from scales. The chords in a major key are derived from a major scale and the chords in a minor key from a minor scale. Let's compare the difference between a C major scale and a C natural minor scale in parallel or from the same root.

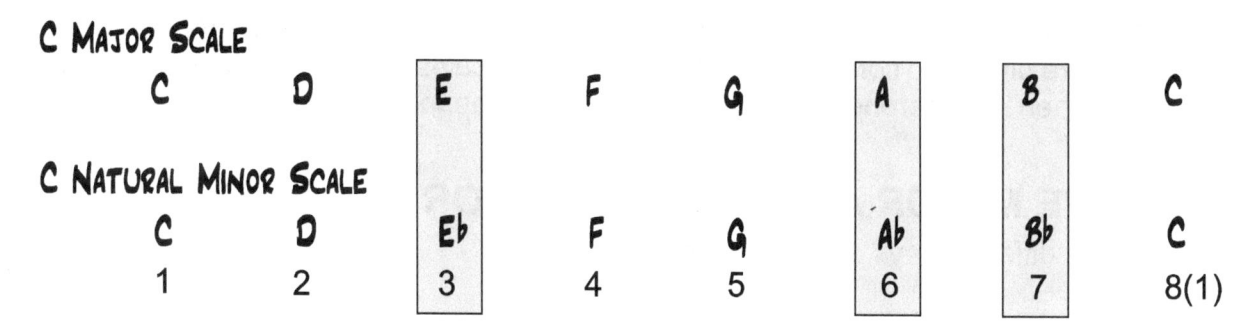

C Major Scale
C   D   E   F   G   A   B   C

C Natural Minor Scale
C   D   Eb F   G   Ab Bb C
1   2   3   4   5   6   7   8(1)

As you can see the natural minor scale has a lowered 3rd degree making it minor and also has a lowered 6th and 7th. If we think of scales as colours we would think of a major scale as a bright colour like orange or yellow, when we lower the 3, 6 and 7 as above, it takes on a cooler shade of blue or green.

The following chords are derived from natural minor.

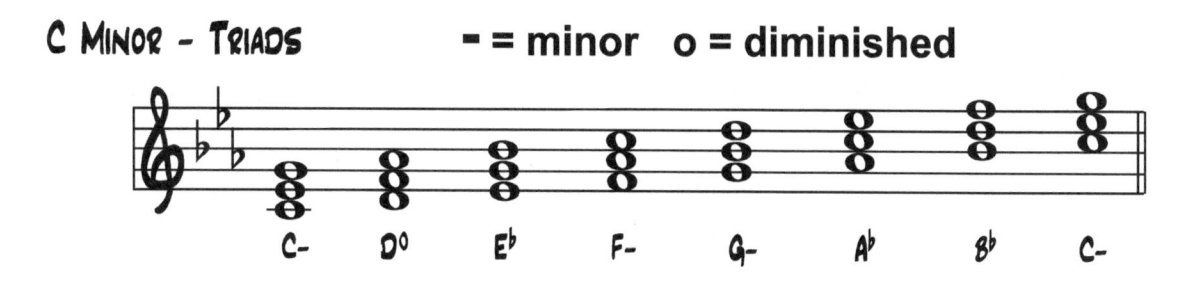

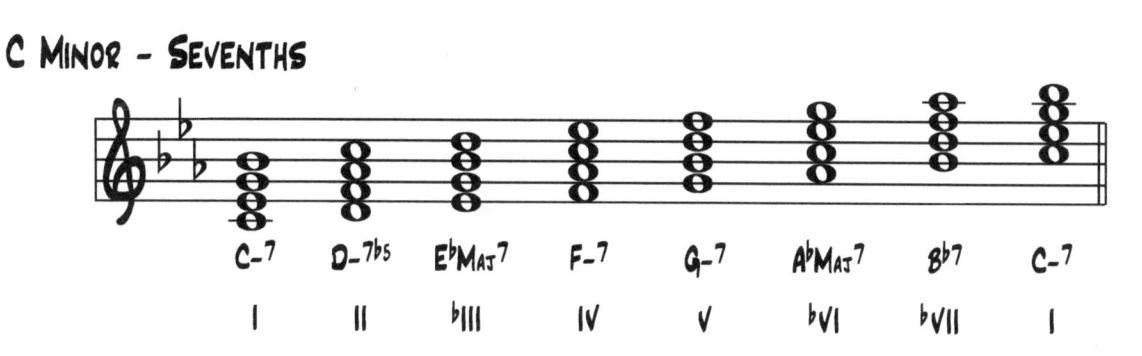

C Minor - Triads   - = minor   o = diminished

C-   D°   Eb   F-   G-   Ab   Bb   C-

C Minor - Sevenths

C-7   D-7b5   EbMaj7   F-7   G-7   AbMaj7   Bb7   C-7
I   II   bIII   IV   V   bVI   bVII I

The II V I progression in a minor key when using 4-note chords as derived from the Natural Minor scale is:

| D-7b5 | G-7 | C- | % |

PARALLEL AND RELATIVE

When we begin the study of Major and Minor sounds we most often learn them relatively but to progress in your understanding of harmony it is important to understand them in Parallel.

Relative scales share the same notes but they do not share the same key or tonal center, so the sounds are difficult to compare. When we view the scales from the same root, tonic or tonal center then the differences in tonality become more apparent.

RELATIVE MAJOR AND NATURAL MINOR
Same notes, different keys or tonal center

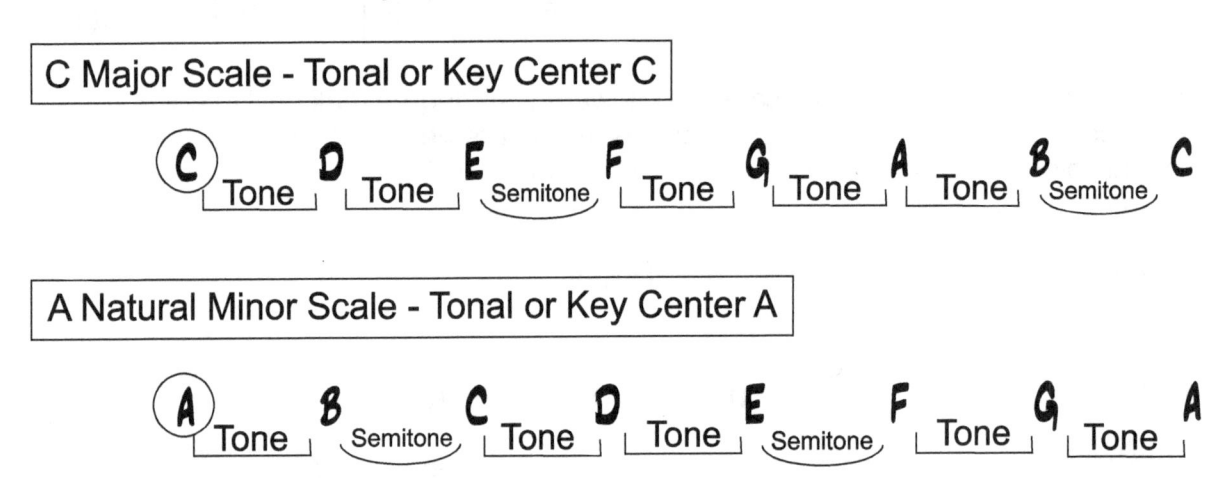

C Major Scale - Tonal or Key Center C

C — Tone — D — Tone — E — Semitone — F — Tone — G — Tone — A — Tone — B — Semitone — C

A Natural Minor Scale - Tonal or Key Center A

A — Tone — B — Semitone — C — Tone — D — Tone — E — Semitone — F — Tone — G — Tone — A

PARALLEL MAJOR AND NATURAL MINOR
Same key or tonal center

C Major Scale - Tonal or Key Center C

C — Tone — D — Tone — E — Semitone — F — Tone — G — Tone — A — Tone — B — Semitone — C

C Natural Minor Scale - Tonal or Key Center C

C — Tone — D — Semitone — E♭ — Tone — F — Tone — G — Semitone — A♭ — Tone — B♭ — Tone — C

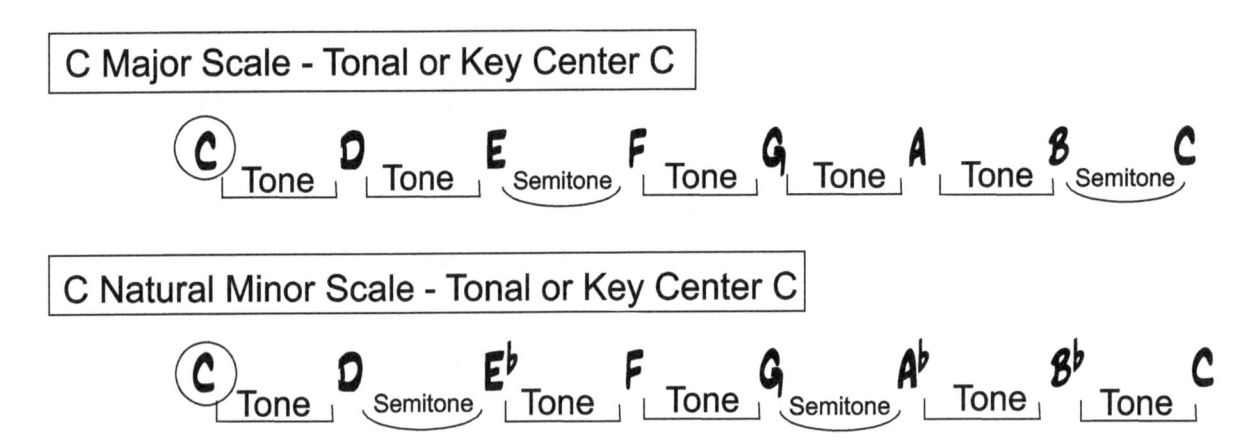

C minor 7

The same principals of deriving chords from a major key also apply to a minor key. Let's begin with the scale of C natural minor:

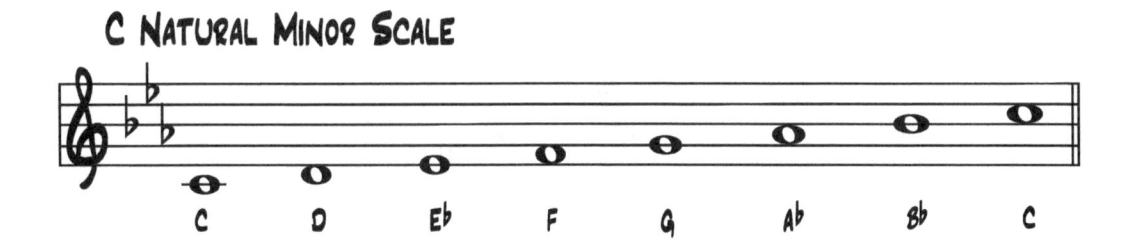

C Natural Minor Scale

C D Eb F G Ab Bb C

Now take the 1 - 3 - 5 of the scale to derive the tonic chord.

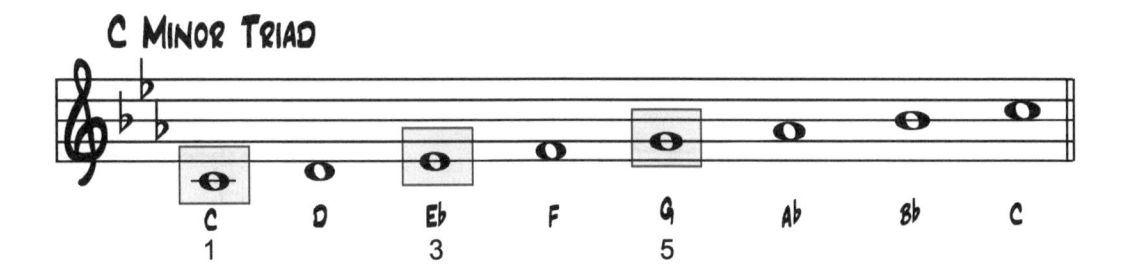

C Minor Triad

C D Eb F G Ab Bb C
1   3   5

Or the 1 - 3 - 5 - 7 of the scale for the C minor 7 chord.

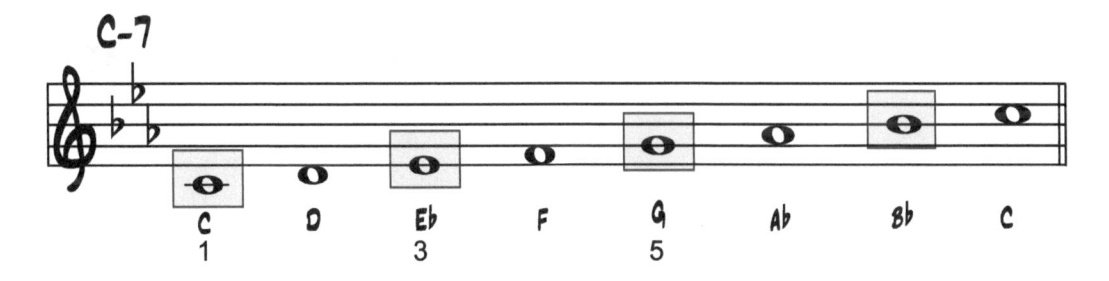

C-7

C D Eb F G Ab Bb C
1   3   5

As you can see the I chord derived from the key of C minor is minor, both as a triad and as a minor 7th or 4-note chord.

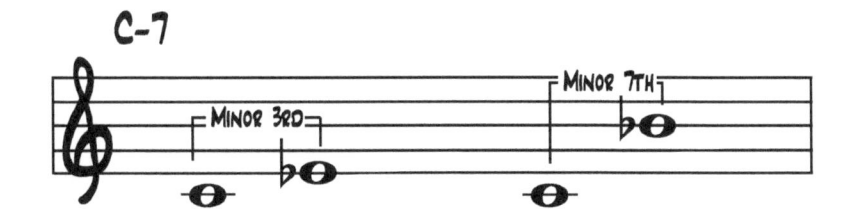

C-7

Minor 3rd — Minor 7th

Let's take a look at this chord on the fretboard.

29

C minor 7
ROOT 6, 5, 2

ARPEGGIO

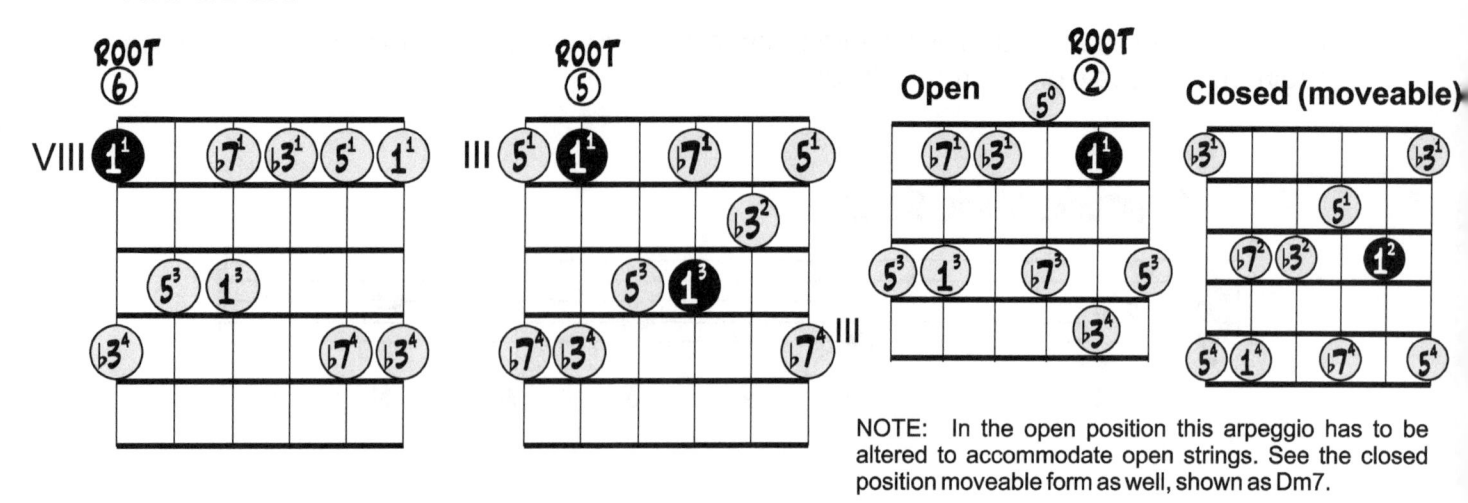

NOTE: In the open position this arpeggio has to be altered to accommodate open strings. See the closed position moveable form as well, shown as Dm7.

CHORD

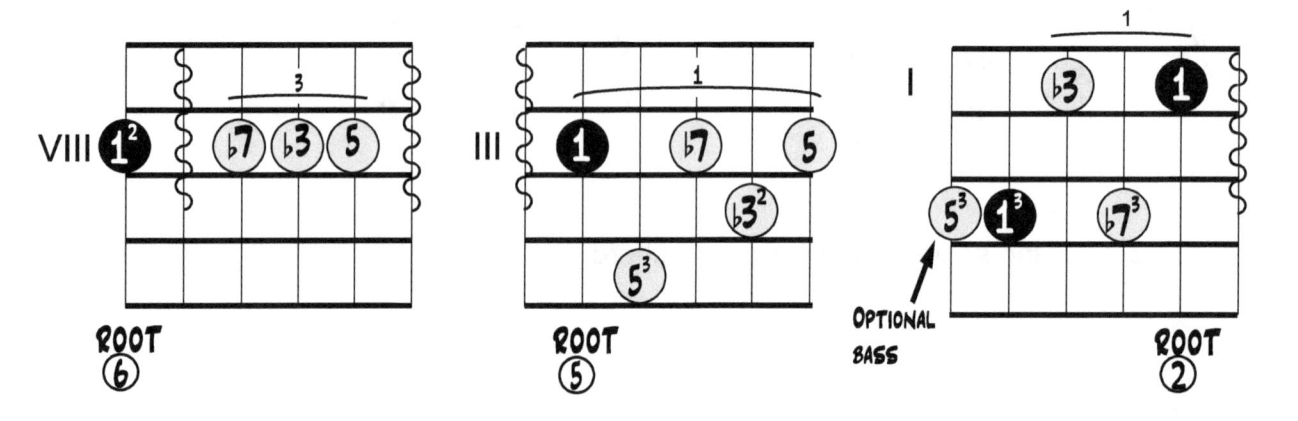

CHORD SPELLING

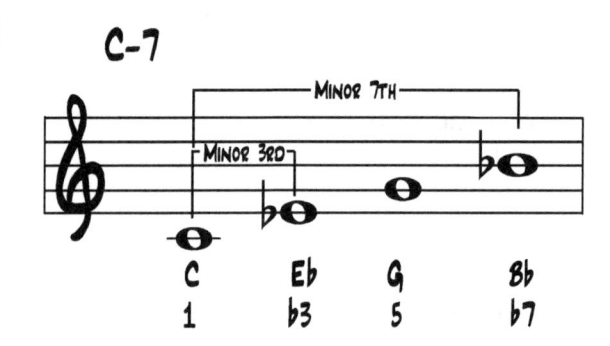

C-7: C (1), Eb (b3), G (5), Bb (b7) — Minor 3rd, Minor 7th

NOTE: All arpeggio forms are moveable but are shown as C-7 in the above diagrams

II CHORD IN A MINOR KEY

The II chord (triad) in a minor key is a diminished chord. If we examine this from the II degree of the C natural minor scale you can see that the V degree of the chord is a ♭5 or diminished 5th. Another way to look at it is that the diminished chord is made up of consecutive minor 3rd intervals.

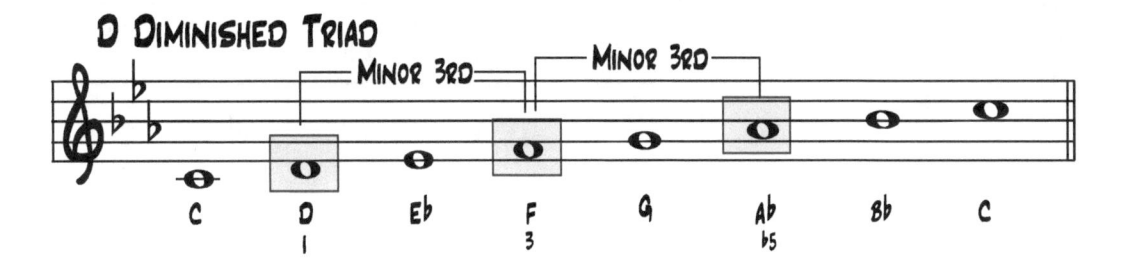

When we add the 7th degree of the II chord, the chord becomes a minor 7♭5 or a half diminished ø. The chord is called half diminished because there is a major 3rd between the 5th and the 7th of the chord and not an additional minor 3rd.

A diminished 7 chord has a lowered 7th or minor 3 between the 5th and 7th; the chord is thus made up entirely of minor 3rds making it fully diminished. This chord is not the II chord in a natural minor scale and will be covered in detail later.

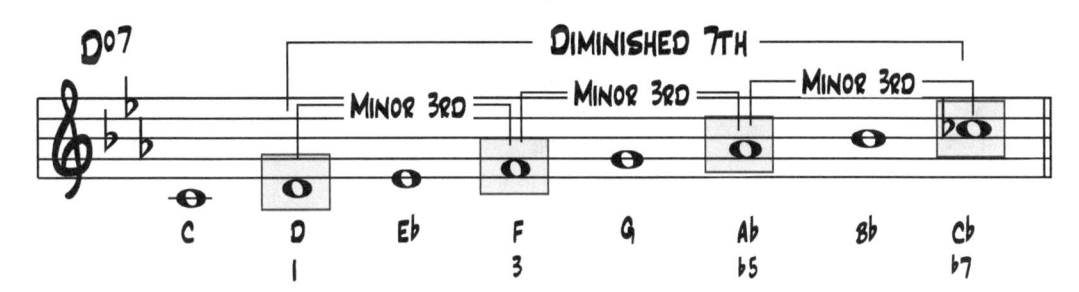

The Dm7♭5 chord or D half diminished is the II chord in a minor key and is often found in the parallel major key, for example:

| D-7♭5 | G7 | Cmaj7 | Cmaj7 |

(minor: D-7♭5 | G7) (Major: Cmaj7 | Cmaj7)

D minor 7♭5

The minor 7♭5 chord can be built from the II degree of the natural minor scale.

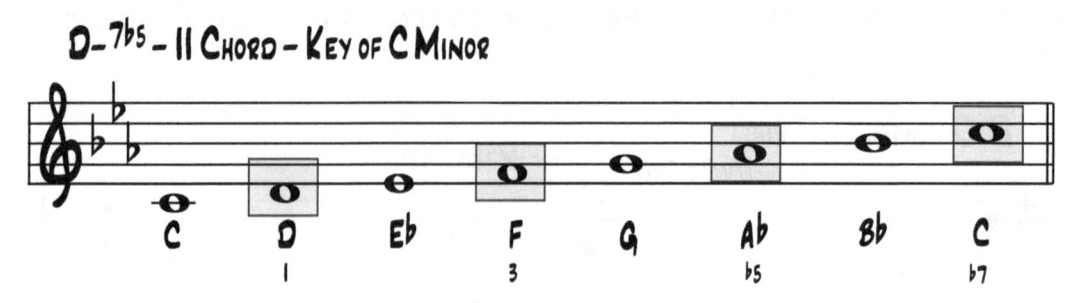

D-7♭5 - II Chord - Key of C Minor

C D E♭ F G A♭ B♭ C
   1   3   ♭5   ♭7

These notes spell a Dm7♭5 chord: D F A♭ C

When we construct the II chord in a minor key we do it in the same way we do other chords, by building in thirds: take - skip - take - skip - take. In the case of the II chord in a minor key we have a ♭5 degree in a minor 7th chord. This ♭5 gives the chord a distinctively dark minor sound.

The m7♭5 is also referred to as a half diminished, using the diminished symbol with a slash ⌀

SPELLINGS IN PARALLEL (SAME ROOT)

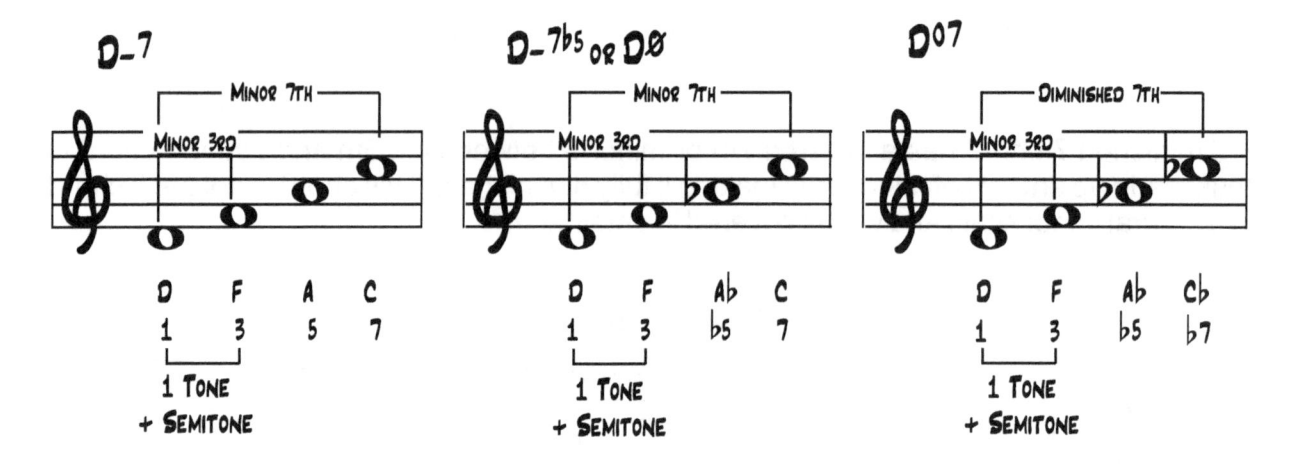

D-7 — Minor 7th / Minor 3rd
D F A C
1 3 5 7
1 Tone + Semitone

D-7♭5 or D⌀ — Minor 7th / Minor 3rd
D F A♭ C
1 3 ♭5 7
1 Tone + Semitone

D°7 — Diminished 7th / Minor 3rd
D F A♭ C♭
1 3 ♭5 ♭7
1 Tone + Semitone

Chord Type	Intervals from Root
Minor 7	min 3, min 7
Minor 7 ♭5	min 3, dim 5, min 7
Diminished 7	min 3, dim 5, dim 7

D minor 7♭5
ROOT 6, 5, 2

ARPEGGIO

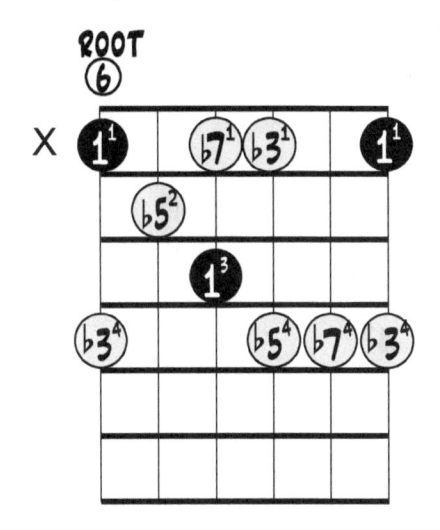

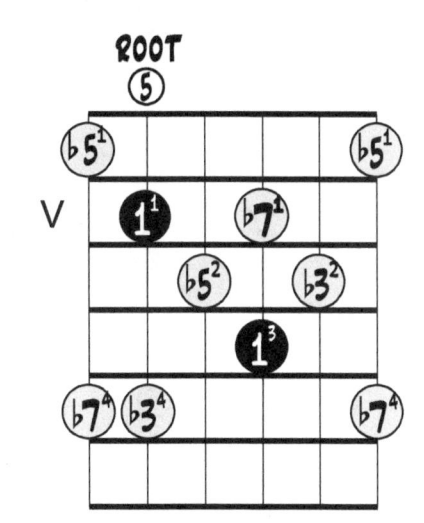

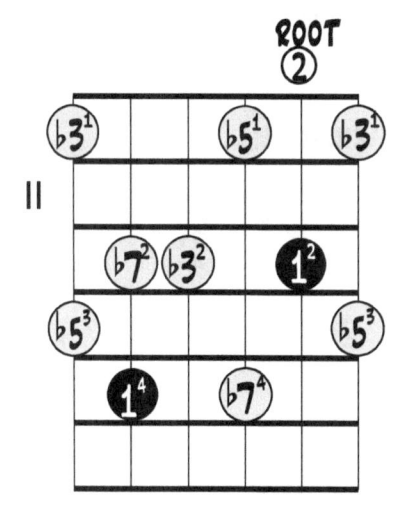

CHORD

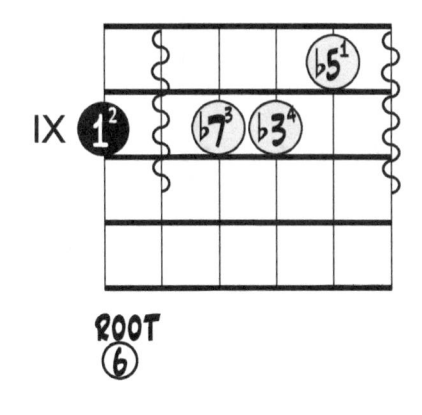

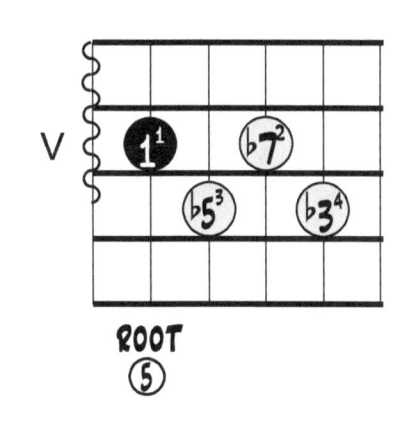

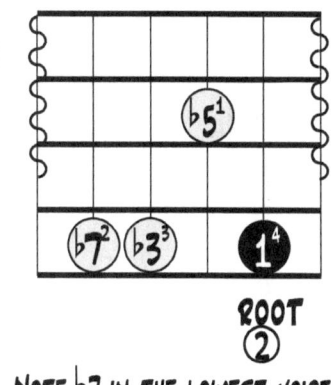

Note ♭7 in the lowest voice

CHORD SPELLING

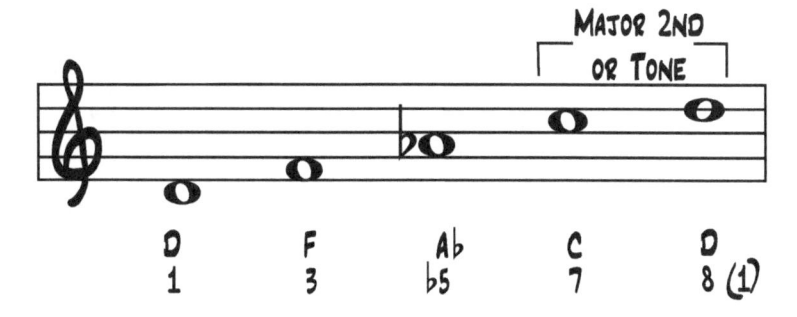

D	F	A♭	C	D
1	3	♭5	7	8 (1)

Major 2nd or Tone (between C and D)

PROGRESSIONS FOR PRACTICE

The following progressions use the minor 7♭5 chord as a II chord. Listen for the moving major to minor 6th within the key and be aware of the movement on the fretboard.

EXERCISE

1. 4/4 ‖: D-7 ⑤ / / / | D-7♭5 ⑤ / / / | G7 ⑥ / / / | Cmaj7 ⑥ / / / :‖

2. 4/4 ‖: D-7♭5 ⑤ / / / | G7 ⑥ / / / | C- ⑤ / / / | A7 ⑥ / / / :‖

3. 4/4 ‖: B- ⑥ / / / | B-7♭5 ⑥ / / / | E7 ⑤ / / / | Amaj7 ⑥ / / / :‖

4. 4/4 ‖: B-7♭5 ⑥ / / / | E7 ⑤ / / / | Amaj7 ⑥ / / / | F#7 ⑥ / / / :‖

5. 4/4 ‖: E-7♭5 ⑤ / / / | A7 ⑥ / / / | D-7 ⑤ / / / | B7 ⑥ / / / :‖

6. 4/4 ‖: E-7 ② / / / | E-7♭5 ② / / / | A7 ⑤ / / / | Dmaj7 ⑤ / / / :‖

7. 4/4 ‖: F-7 ⑤ / / / | F-7♭5 ⑤ / / / | B♭7 ⑥ / / / | E♭maj7 ⑤ / / / :‖

8. 4/4 ‖: G-7♭5 ② / / / | C7 ⑥ / / / | Fmaj7 ⑤ / / / | D7 ⑤ / / / :‖

9. 4/4 ‖: E♭-7♭5 ⑤ / / / | A♭7 ⑥ / / / | D♭maj7 ⑤ / / / | G♭maj7 ⑥ / / / :‖

10. 4/4 ‖: C-7♭5 ⑤ / / / | F7 ⑤ / / / | B♭-7 ⑥ / / / | G7 ⑥ / / / :‖

Note the root on 2nd string chord form has the 7th in the lowest voice in this case. Follow the suggested roots to start and then try some alternatives.

Play-along tracks are available at **www.MyGuitarPal.com**.

THE HARMONIC MINOR SCALE
The 7♭9 Chord

The natural minor scale has a minor V chord which has a rather weak resolution to the I chord. To correct this the 7th of the scale is raised to produce a major V chord or a V7 chord with a strong leading tone to the Tonic of the key.

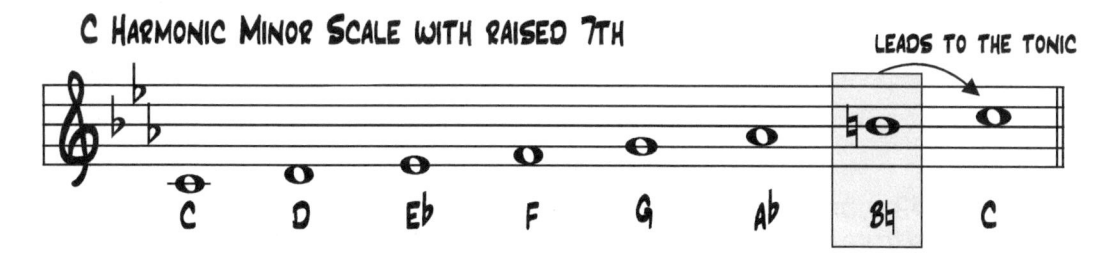

When we now derive a V chord from the harmonic minor scale it produces a major triad

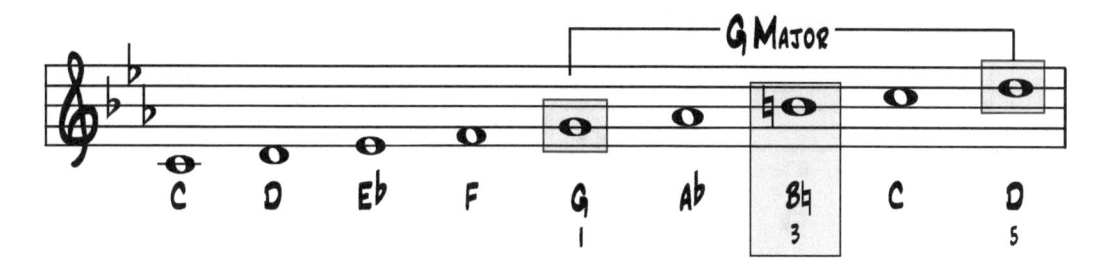

The 4-note chord yields a dominant-type 7 chord with a major 3rd and minor 7th from the root.

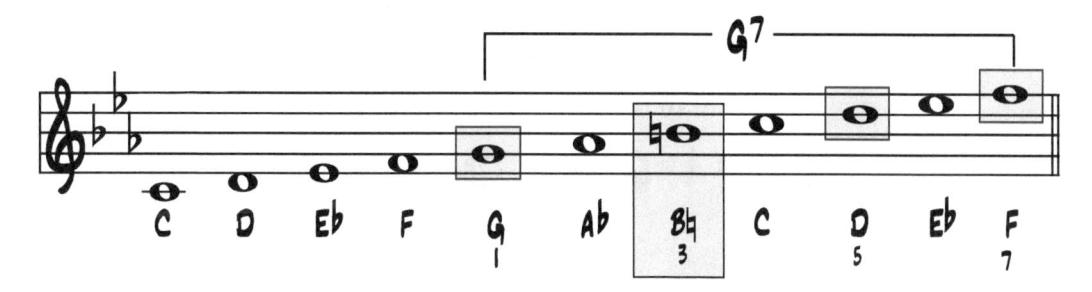

The 9th degree of the chord will be a ♭9 and thus yield a 7♭9 chord which is a strong characteristic harmony of the minor key. Note that the root of G and the ♭9 or A♭ are a semitone apart.

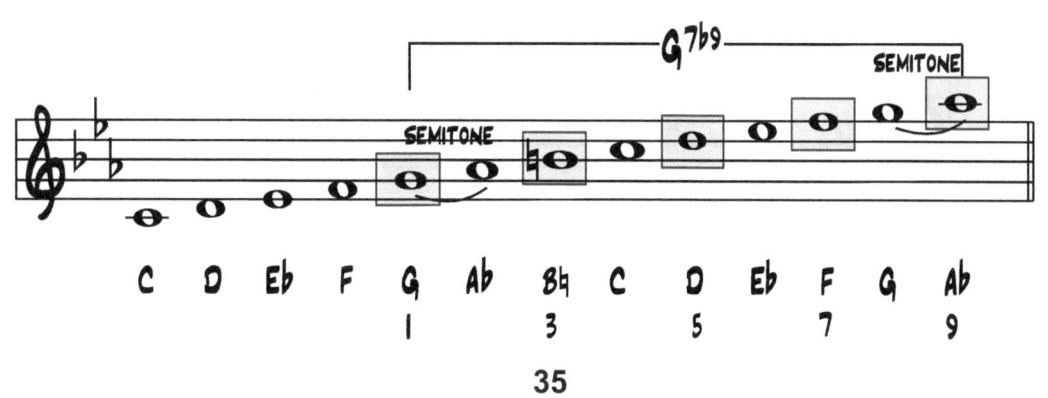

7♭9 ARPEGGIO

The 7♭9 chord begins with a major triad.

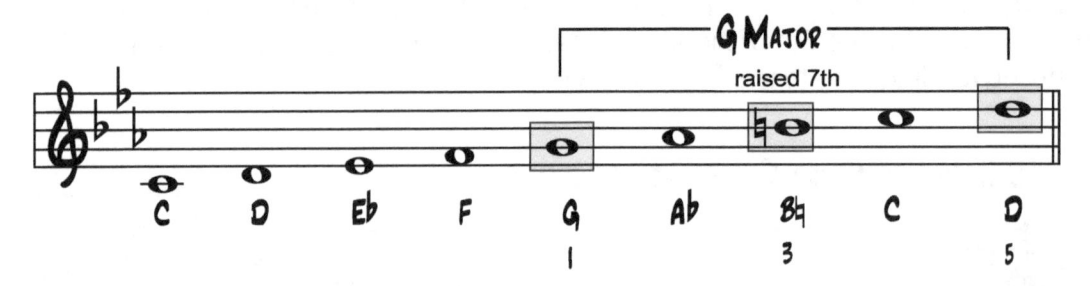

The notes in a G7♭9 chord are: G - B - D - F - A♭, or root, 3rd, 5th, 7 and ♭9. Note that the ♭9 is a semitone away from the tonic. In voicing a 7♭9 chord it is common to eliminate either the root or the 5th of the chord.

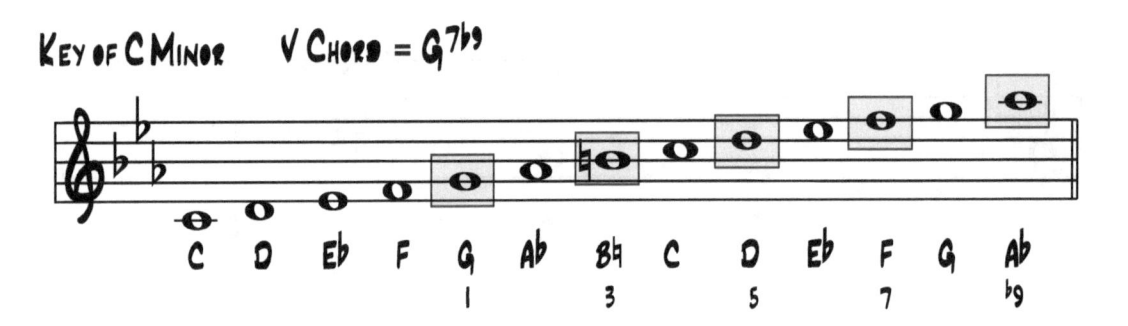

The 7♭9 chord is often used in place of the common 7th chord due to its characteristic minor quality and added harmonic complexity.

| D-7♭5 | G7♭9 | CMaj7 | A7 |

— derived from minor —

The 7♭9 adds further harmonic possibilities for parallel and composite major and minor keys.

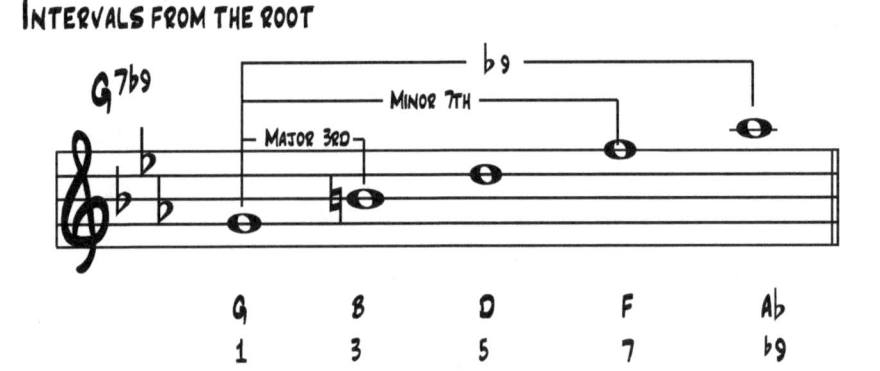

Let's examine this sound on the fretboard.

36

G7♭9
ROOT 6, 5, 2

ARPEGGIO

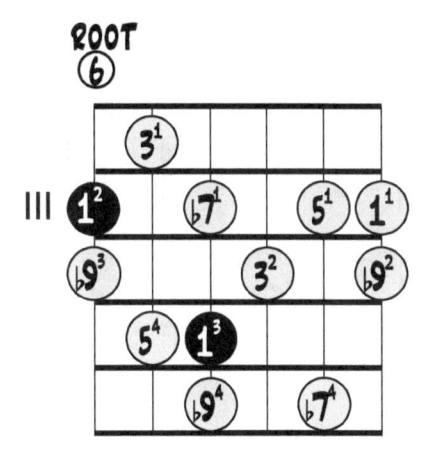

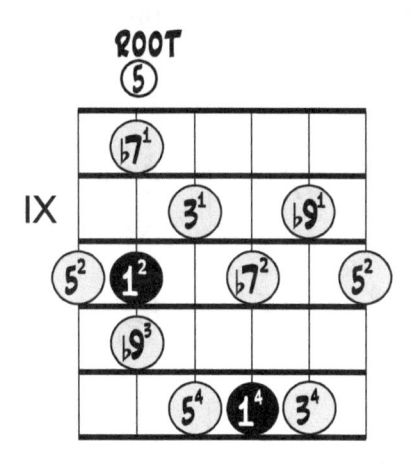

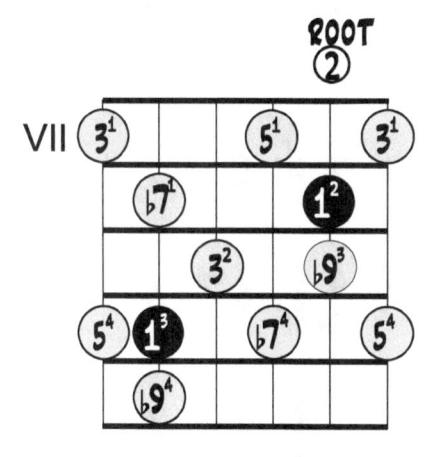

CHORD

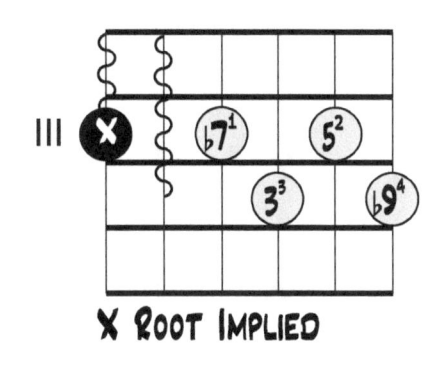

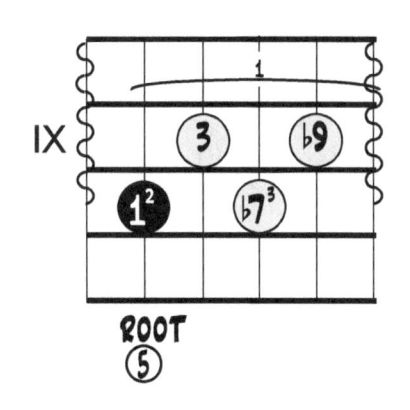

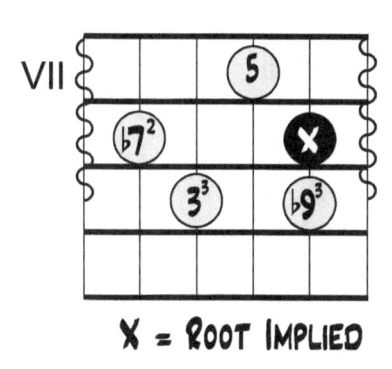

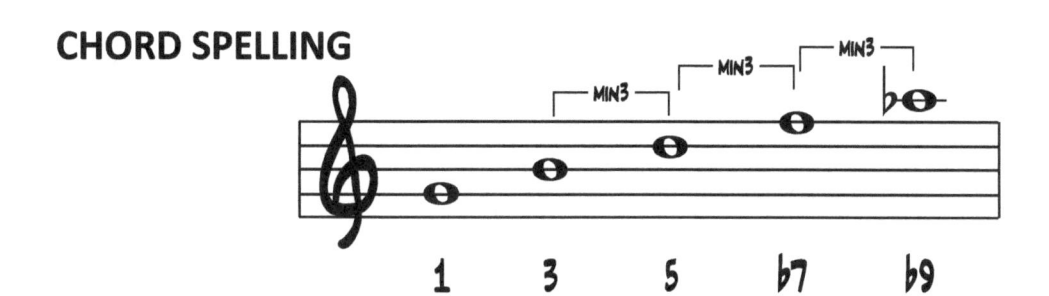

CHORD SPELLING

1 3 5 ♭7 ♭9

NOTE: The top three notes of a 7 chord form a diminished triad. A 7♭9 chord with no root is a dim7 chord. All arpeggio forms are moveable but are shown as G7♭9 in the above diagrams.

PROGRESSIONS FOR PRACTICE

The following progressions use the chord sounds covered thus far and use chords derived from both major and minor scales thus creating composite major and minor progressions.

	II	V	I		Key
1	D-7b5 (5)	G7b9 (6)	Cmaj7 (5)	%	C
2	B-7b5 (5)	E7b9 (6)	A-7 (5)	%	A-
3	A-7b5 (6)	D7b9 (5)	Gmaj7 (6)	%	G
4	F#-7b5 (6)	B7b9 (5)	E-7 (6)	%	E-
5	E-7b5 (5)	A7b9 (6)	Dmaj7 (5)	%	D
6	C#-7b5 (2)	F7b9 (2)	B-7 (5)	%	B-
7	B-7b5 (5)	E7b9 (2)	Amaj7 (6)	%	A
8	Ab-7b5 (6)	Db7b9 (5)	Gb-7 (6)	%	Gb
9	F#-7b5 (2)	B7b9 (2)	Emaj7 (5)	%	E
10	D#-7b5 (2)	G#7b9 (6)	C#-7 (5)	%	C#-

Examine some Real Book standards for II V I progressions in major and minor and composite major/minor. Do your own analysis of some of these standards.

HARMONIC, MELODIC, JAZZ MINOR SCALES

When the 7th degree of the natural minor scale is raised it produces the harmonic minor scale yielding a major triad or dominant 7 chord on the V degree of the scale. Raising the 7th degree creates an augmented 2nd between degrees 6 and 7. Melodically the augmented 2nd produces a middle eastern sound which is not always desirable so the scale can be altered to correct this.

C Harmonic Minor Scale

C D Eb F G Ab B♮ C

To close the augmented second interval between 6 and 7, the 6th is also raised thereby creating the melodic minor scale. Due to the fact that the raised 6 and 7 cause the scale to have considerable forward motion this can be mitigated by descending natural minor.

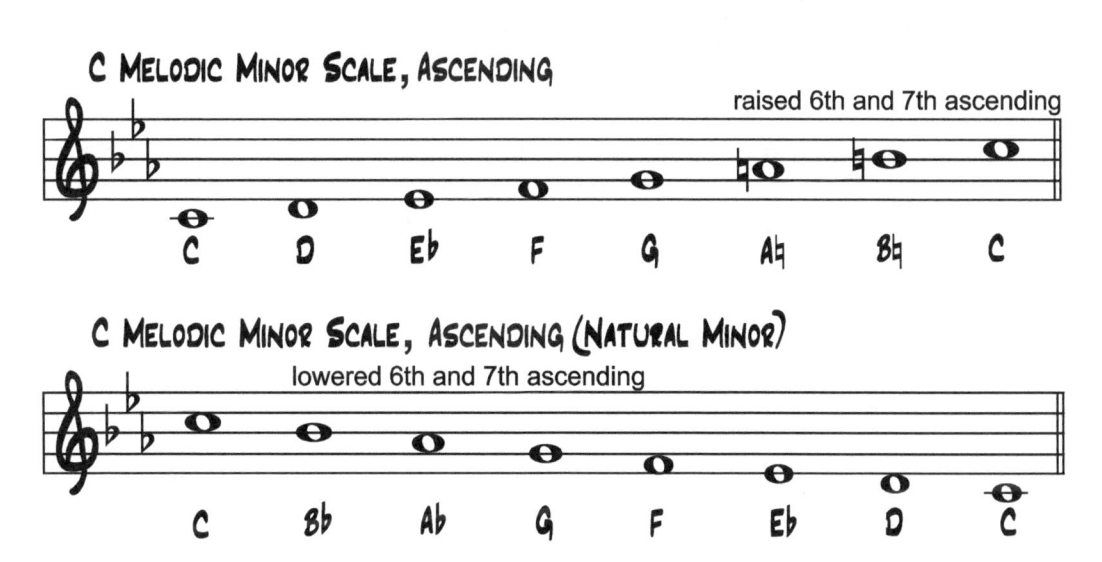

C Melodic Minor Scale, Ascending

raised 6th and 7th ascending

C D Eb F G A♮ B♮ C

C Melodic Minor Scale, Ascending (Natural Minor)

lowered 6th and 7th ascending

C Bb Ab G F Eb D C

The so-called jazz minor scale ascends and descends with the same raised 6 and 7 degrees. The same result can be produced by simply lowering the 3rd degree of a major scale.

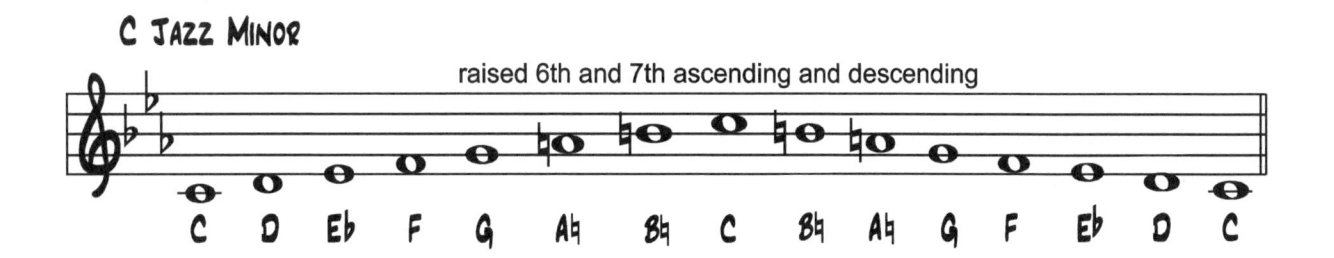

C Jazz Minor

raised 6th and 7th ascending and descending

C D Eb F G A♮ B♮ C B♮ A♮ G F Eb D C

COMPOSITE HARMONY

When we combine the scales of major and natural minor we arrive at a composite major/minor scale. The chords constructed from each of the two scales will be combined and named according to all of the scale degrees in both scales. These scale degrees are named according to how they would be altered in the major scale, using the major scale as the reference scale.

	I	II	♭III	III	IV	V	♭VI	VI	♭VII	VII
C Major	Cmaj7	D-7		E-7	Fmaj7	G7		A-7		B-7♭5
C Natural Minor	C-7	D-7♭5	E♭maj7		F-7	G-7	A♭maj7		B♭7	
Expanded Key of C	I / C	II / D	♭III / E♭	III / E	IV / F	V / G	♭VI / A♭	VI / A	♭VII / B♭	VII / B

The chord names with their root designations and functions in C would now include a ♭III major, ♭VI major and ♭VII major as well as some additional sounds added to the major tonality as I, IV and V minor and m7♭5. These additions to the harmonic palette considerably increase the possibilities within a key.

Remember that C is still the tonal centre.

Harmonizations of the scales can be compared in the same way. Let's take the I, II and V chords built on these degrees as an example; for the sake of this study we will make these chords 7ths and in the case of the V chord in minor we will go as far as the 9th.

The composite I, II and V chords in the now broader composite key of C would be:

Composite Key	I Chord	II Chord	V7 Chord
C Major/Cminor	Cmaj7/Cm7	Dm7/Dm7♭5	G7/7♭9

This logic of composite and parallel keys should bring us to a new understanding of the definition of "key."

COMPOSITE PROGRESSIONS

The following progressions are examples of composite major and minor harmony in common use - all are in the key of C. Note that the G7b9 is borrowed from the harmonic minor scale.

1. $\|$: D-7 / / / (IIm) | B♭7 / / / (♭VII) | Cmaj7 / / / (IMaj) | % :$\|$

2. $\|$: E♭maj7 / / / (♭VIIIMaj) | D-7♭5 / / / (IIm) | G7♭9 / / / (Vm) | Cmaj7 / / / (I) :$\|$

3. $\|$: Cmaj7 / / / (I) | Fmaj7 / / / (IV) | F-7 / / / (IVm) | Cmaj7 / / / (I) :$\|$

4. $\|$: Cmaj7 / / / (I) | A♭maj7 / / / (♭VIMaj) | G7 / / / (V) | Cmaj7 / / / (I) :$\|$

5. $\|$: C-7 / / / (I-) | F-7 / / / (IV-) | G7♭9 / / / (V7♭9) | Cmaj7 / / / (I) :$\|$

6. $\|$: C-7 / / / (I) | F-7 / / / (IV) | G-7 / / / (V) | Cmaj7 / / / (I) :$\|$

7. $\|$: Cmaj7 / / / (I) | E♭maj7 / / / (♭IIIMaj) | D-7 / / / (II) | D-7♭5 / / / (II-) :$\|$

8. $\|$: E♭maj7 / / / (♭III) | A♭maj7 / / / (♭VI) | G7 / / / (V) | Cmaj7 / / / (I) :$\|$

Although the scope of this book does not allow for an indepth study of harmony the above progressions will nevertheless provide a better understanding of the myriad harmonic possibilities in composite harmony.

Try transposing the same sounds to other keys.

NIGHT AND DAY
Harmonic Analysis

A

II	V	I	
D-7b5 / / /	G7 / / /	Cmaj7 / / /	%

II	V	I	
D-7b5 / / /	G7 / / /	Cmaj7 / / /	%

II of E-	IV-	III	Passing°
F#-7b5 / / /	F-7 / / /	E-7 / / /	Eb°7

II	V	I	
D-7b5 / / /	G7 / / /	Cmaj7 / / /	%

B

bIII Maj (relative to C-)		I	
EbMaj7 / / /	%	Cmaj7 / / /	%

bIII Maj (relative to C-)		I	
EbMaj7 / / /	%	Cmaj7 / / /	%

II of E-	IV-	III	Passing°
F#-7b5 / / /	F-7 / / /	E-7 / / /	Eb°7

II	V	I	
D-7 / / /	G7 / / /	Cmaj7 / / /	%

NOTE: In the above standard we resolve to Cmaj but use the II and the V chords from the key of C minor. In the B section the Eb major is the relative major of C minor or the bIII major in a composite key. This progression is a good example of composite and parallel major and minor.

As of yet we have not visited the diminished chord and its function so for the time being it will suffice to identify it simply as a passing diminished.

Section 4

DIMINISHED AND ALTERED DOMINANTS

Tension leading toward resolution

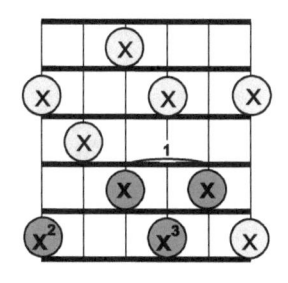

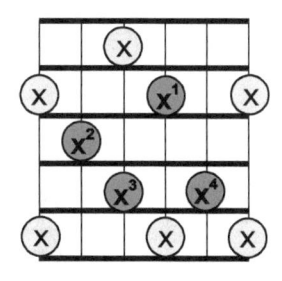

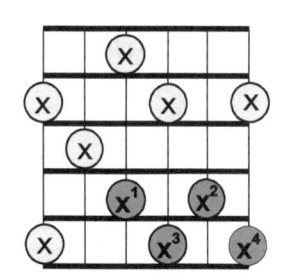

DIMINISHED 7 CHORD

The diminished chord functions as a dominant sound, in fact the top three notes of a dominant 7 chord are a diminished triad so we can think of a diminished chord as a 7th with an implied root. The diminished 7th adds another minor 3rd and can function as a 7♭9 with an implied root. The notes of a 7♭9 can be derived from a minor scale. Let's examine the basic theory:

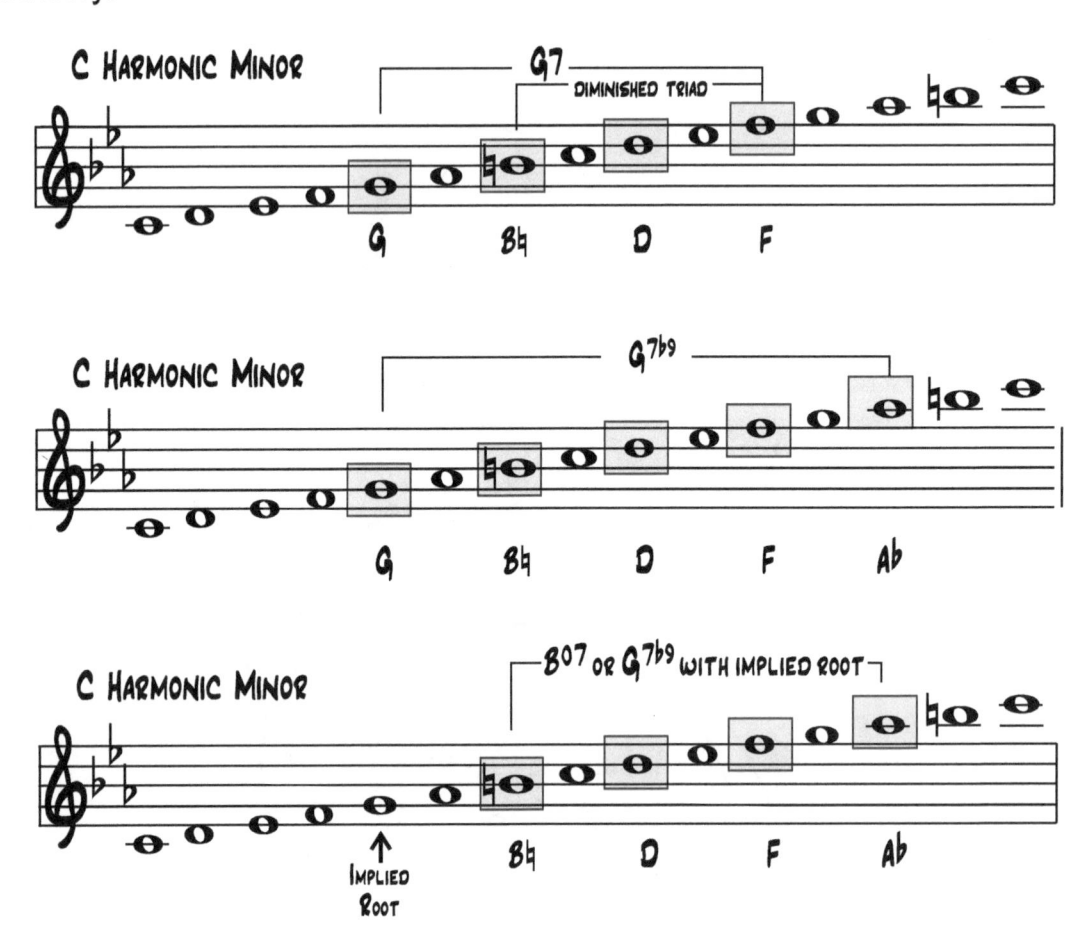

The diminished arpeggio is an equal division of the octave into minor 3rds, because of this there is no harmonic hierarchy within a diminished chord. Therefore, any note in a diminished 7 chord can function as its root note or naming note.

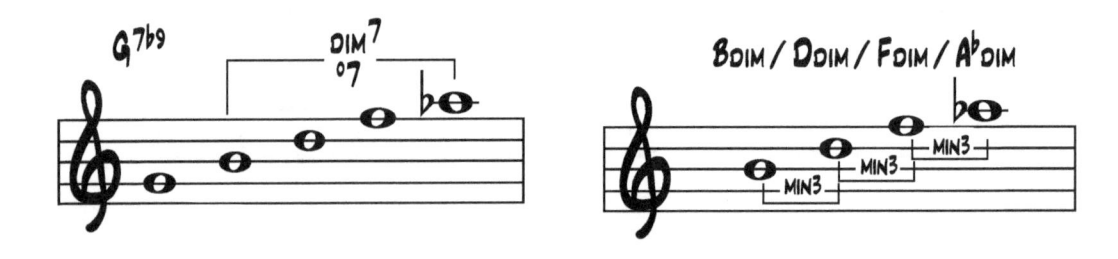

Because of this, the diminished chord wanders in search of resolution.

DIMINISHED 7 ARPEGGIO

Because the diminished chord is an equal division of the octave into equal distances it behaves in somewhat uncanny ways on the fretboard.

Essentially there is only need for one form of a diminished arpeggio which then simply repeats itself every three frets. While you are wrapping your head around that, here is the arpeggio with some related common diminished chord forms.

Remember that diminished chords can function as a dominant chord with no root.

NOTE: With diminished chords any note can be a root note.

This same arpeggio form is used to derive the following dim7 chords.

DIM7 CHORDS

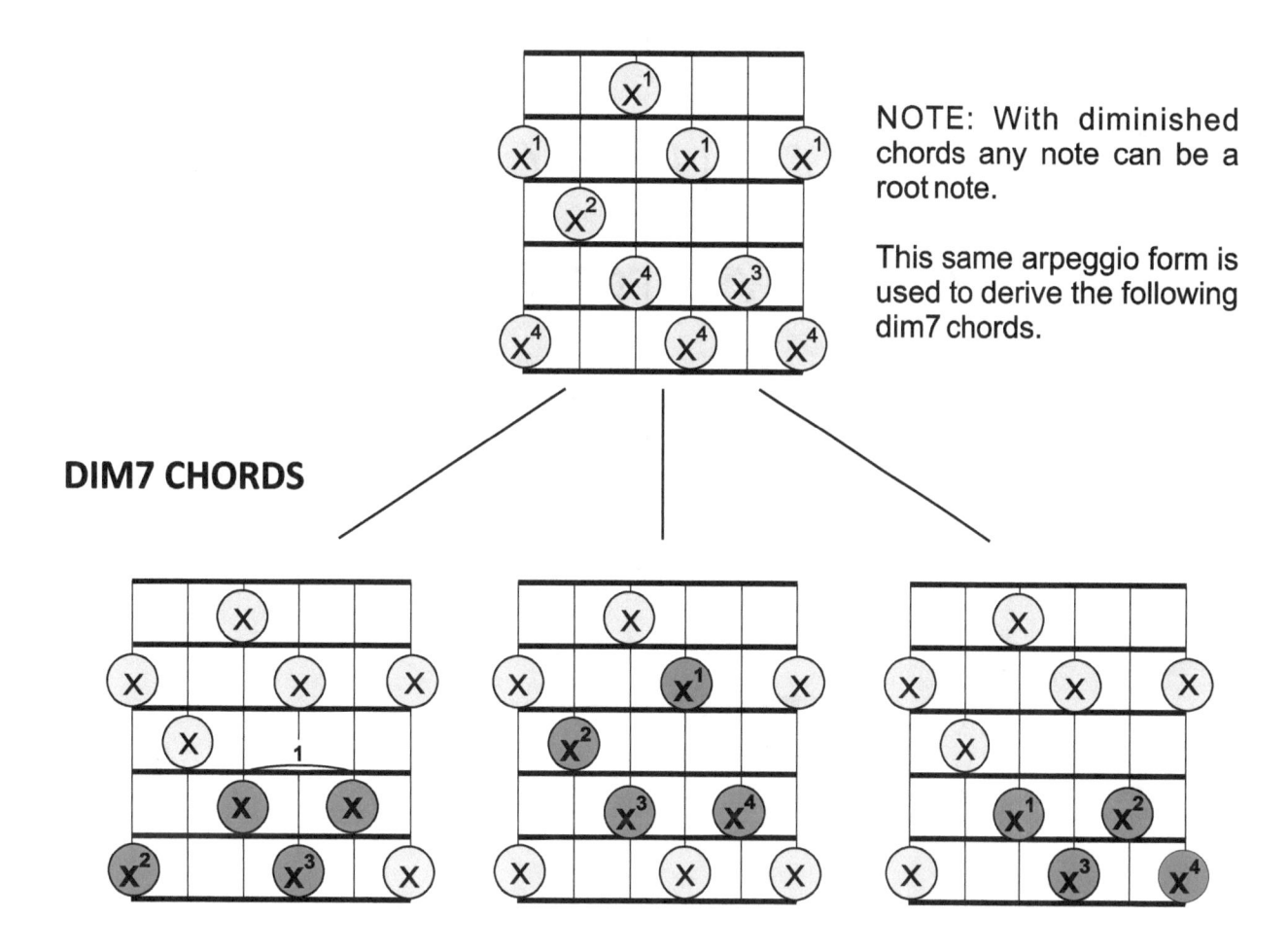

CHORD SPELLING

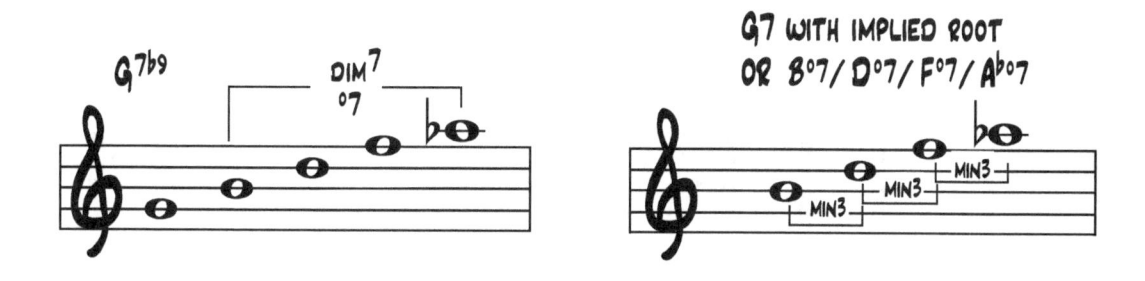

PROGRESSIONS FOR PRACTICE

Try each progression in several positions. Note that diminished chords often pass chromatically to diatonic chords.

1. $\frac{4}{4}$ ‖: CMaj7 / / / | C#o7 / / / | D-7 / / / | G7 / / / :‖

2. $\frac{4}{4}$ ‖: CMaj7 / / / | C7 / / / | F / / / | F#o7 / / / :‖

3. $\frac{4}{4}$ ‖: CMaj7 / / / | C#o7 / / / | D-7 / / / | D#o7 / / / | E- / / / :‖

4. $\frac{4}{4}$ ‖: E-7 / / / | Eo7 / / / | D-7 / / / | Do7 / / / :‖

5. $\frac{4}{4}$ ‖: CMaj7 / / / | Ebo7 / / / | D-7 / / / | G7 / / / :‖

The diminished 7 chord can be used as a substitute for the dominant 7 chord.

‖: D-7 / / / | [G7b9 ROOT IMPLIED — ALL THE SAME CHORD: Fo7 Do7 / Bbo7 Abo7] | CMaj7 / / / | A7 / / / :‖

‖: A-7 / / / | [D7b9 ROOT IMPLIED: Ebo7 Ao7 / F#o7 Co7] | GMaj7 / / / | E7 / / / :‖

‖: E-7 / / / | [A7b9 ROOT IMPLIED: Bbo7 Dbo7 / Go7 Eo7] | DMaj7 / / / | B7 / / / :‖

NOTE: Listen to each of these progressions carefully and try moving to different keys.

ALTERED DOMINANT SOUNDS

The V7 chord can be altered in a number of different ways to add movement and tension. The notes that are commonly altered are the 5 and 9 of the chord. Altering the 5th will result in these chord spellings.

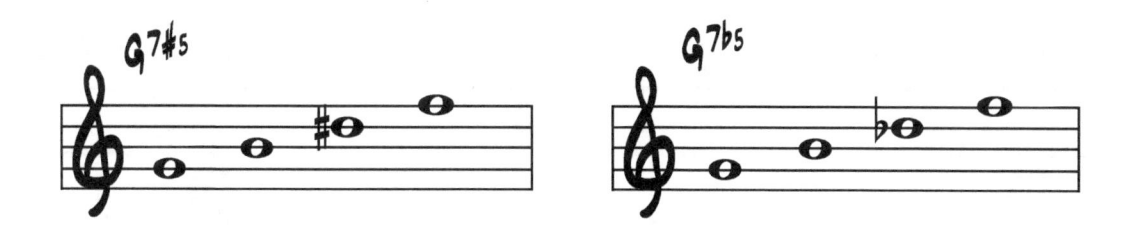

G7#5

G7b5

The raising and lowering of the 9th produces the following spellings:

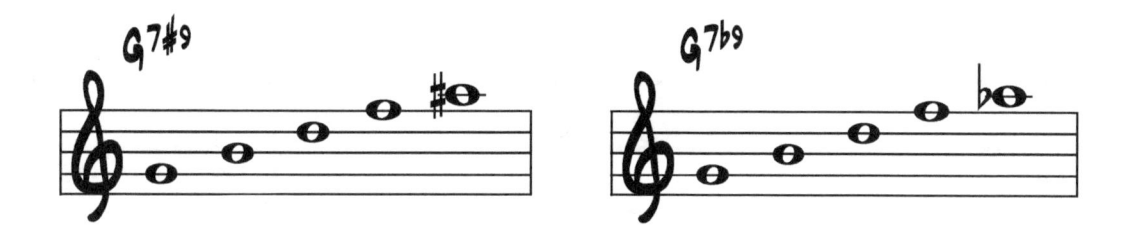

G7#9

G7b9

These same alterations can be used in combination as:

G7#5b9   G7b5b9   G7#5#9   G7b5#9

As far as the arpeggio forms on the guitar are concerned these altered notes can simply be added to the dominant 7 arpeggio forms to create the alterations. These altered dominant arpeggio sounds begin to strongly suggest certain scale sounds as well. It should be noted that these sounds are often associated with Jazz and may not be suitable for all styles, let your ear be your guide.

Each of these altered sounds will be colors to be added in the V7 chord position as:

```
    II        V         I
||: D-7  |  G7 Alt  |  Cmaj7  |  %  :||
```

On the following pages you will find some altered chord forms as well as their related arpeggios. Try spelling your own voicings.

G7#5 OR AUGMENTED 7
ROOT 6, 5, 2

ARPEGGIO

CHORD

CHORD SPELLING

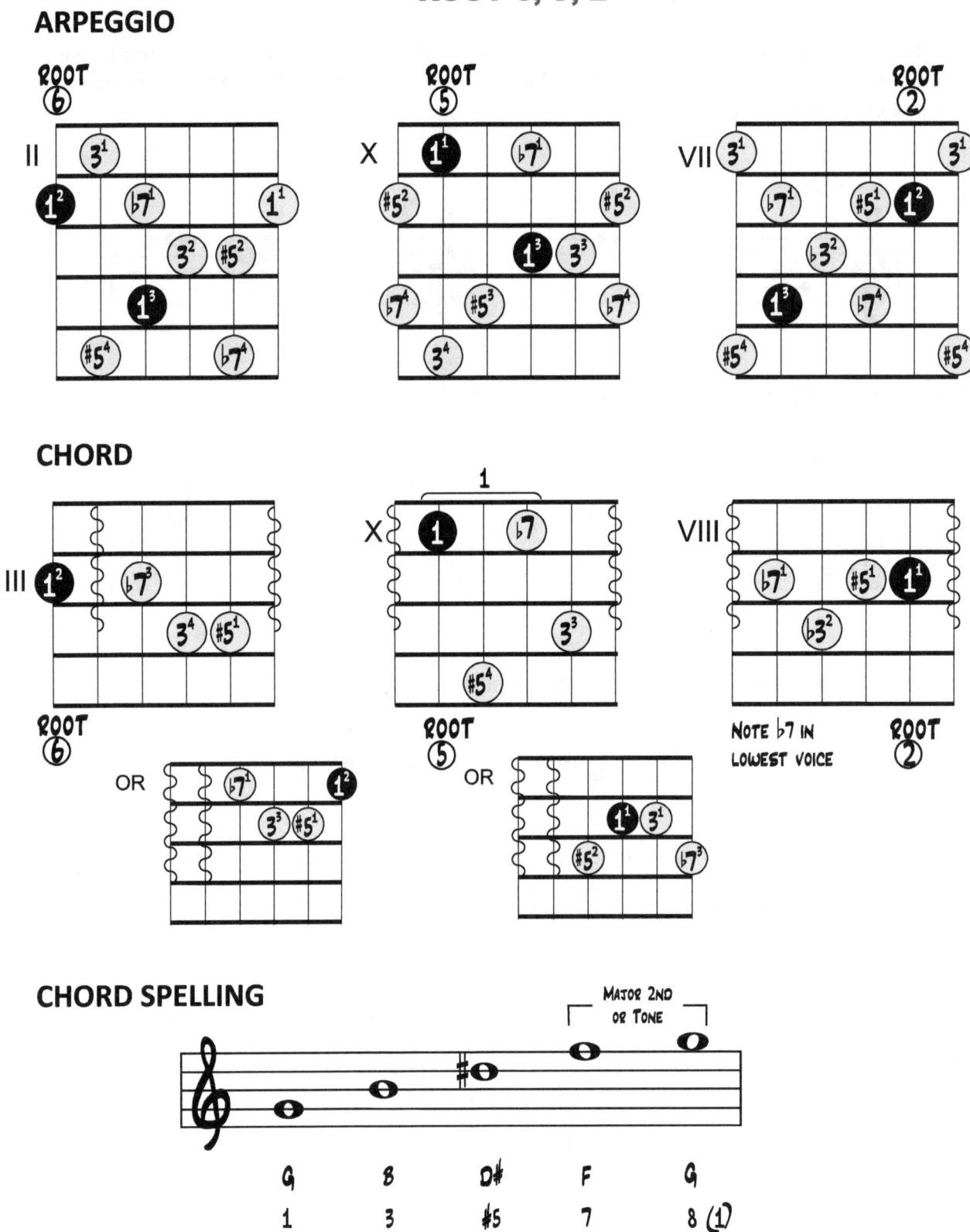

G	B	D#	F	G
1	3	#5	7	8 (1)

Major 2nd or Tone (between F and G)

NOTE: All arpeggio forms are moveable but are shown as G in the above diagrams

G7♭5
ROOT 6, 5, 2

ARPEGGIO

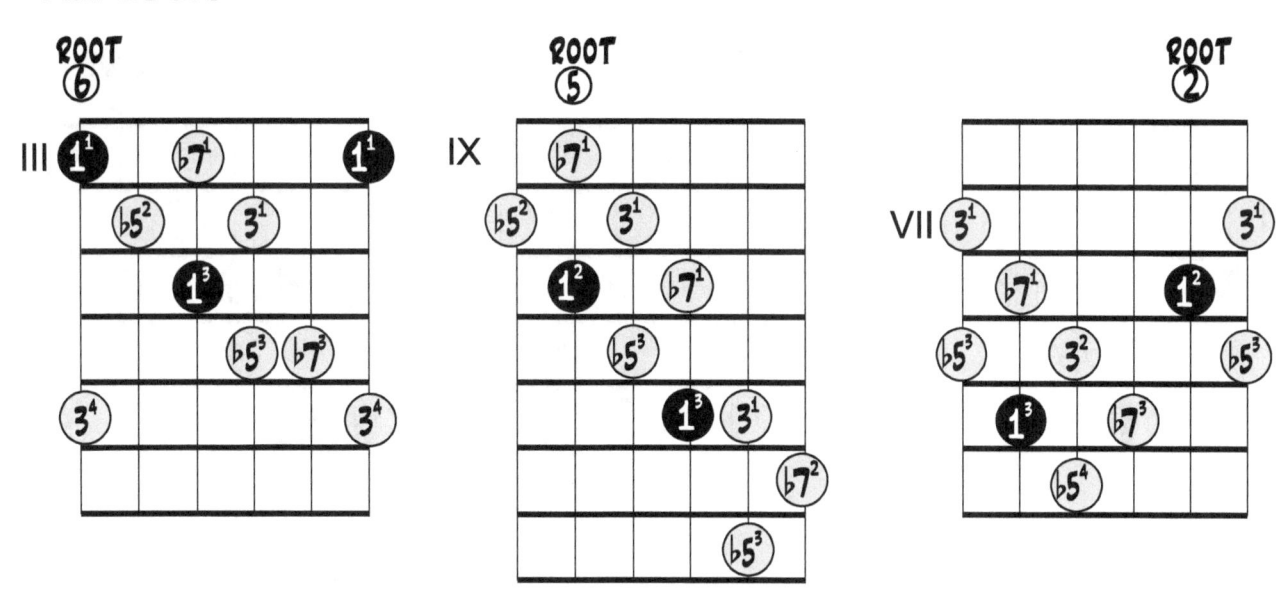

CHORD

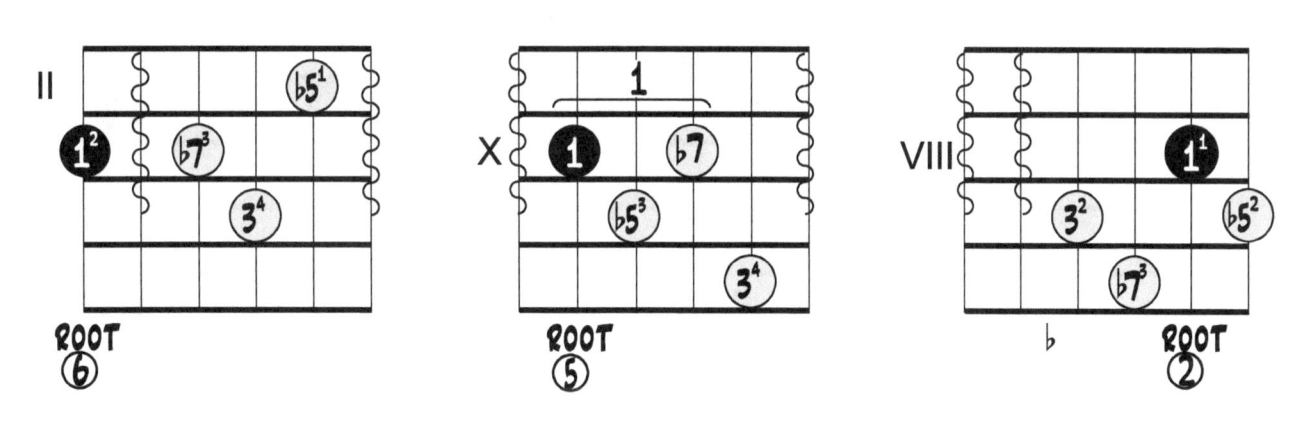

CHORD SPELLING

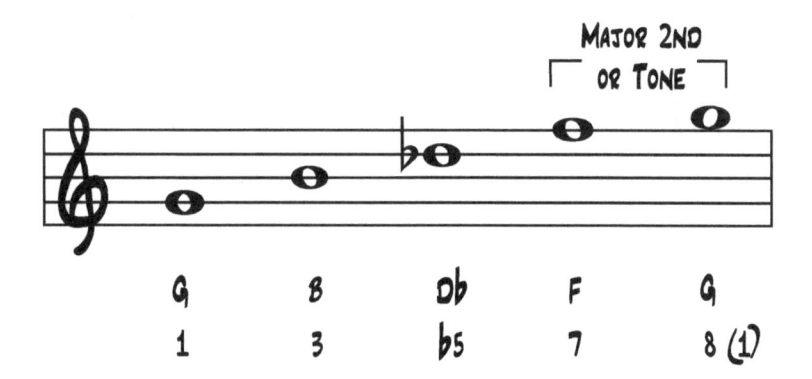

G	B	D♭	F	G
1	3	♭5	7	8 (1)

Major 2nd or Tone (between F and G)

G7♯9
ROOT 6, 5, 2

ARPEGGIO

CHORD

CHORD SPELLING

G	A♯/B♭	B	D	F	A♯
1	♭3	3	5	7	♯9

The ♯9 sound presents some challenges in voicing as it it essentially a minor 3rd against a major 3rd. The minor 3rd is enharmonic with the ♯9. These voicings capture the bite of this chord nicely.

Section 5

ROOT ON STRINGS 3 & 4

Chords and Arpeggios

This section of the book will focus on the root 3 and 4 chord and arpeggio voicings. Thus far we have examined roots, 6, 5 and 2 because these are the most common. This new series of chords and arpeggios will provide a comprehensive and integrated view of the entire fretboard.

For the guitarist with some degree of perseverance this section will provide chords built from every string thus providing a more comprehensive view of useful chords and arpeggio forms in all regions of the fretboard.

THE CAGED SYSTEM
Fretboard Mechanics

Understanding the CAGED system is essential to understanding how the guitar fretboard is organized. The word CAGED is derived from the five basic open chord forms with the same names.

For example, in order to play a C major chord in five positions, these basic open position chords are moved to five regions of the fretboard. This same logic holds true for every chord form.

For example, if we begin with the C Major chord in open position, the chord shapes that follow will be A-G-E-D. When each of these open position chords is played with a C root, they will form C chords across the entire fretboard.

Imagine the fretboard as a conveyor belt of notes. All the forms remain in the same relationships and move in this same fixed relationship across the entire fretboard no matter what the key. Imagine also that the conveyor belt begins to turn around at fret XII to return back to open position.

Examine the following diagrams with care and attention until you begin to understand the logic. I can't over-emphasize the importance of this chapter.

CAGED SYSTEM FROM C

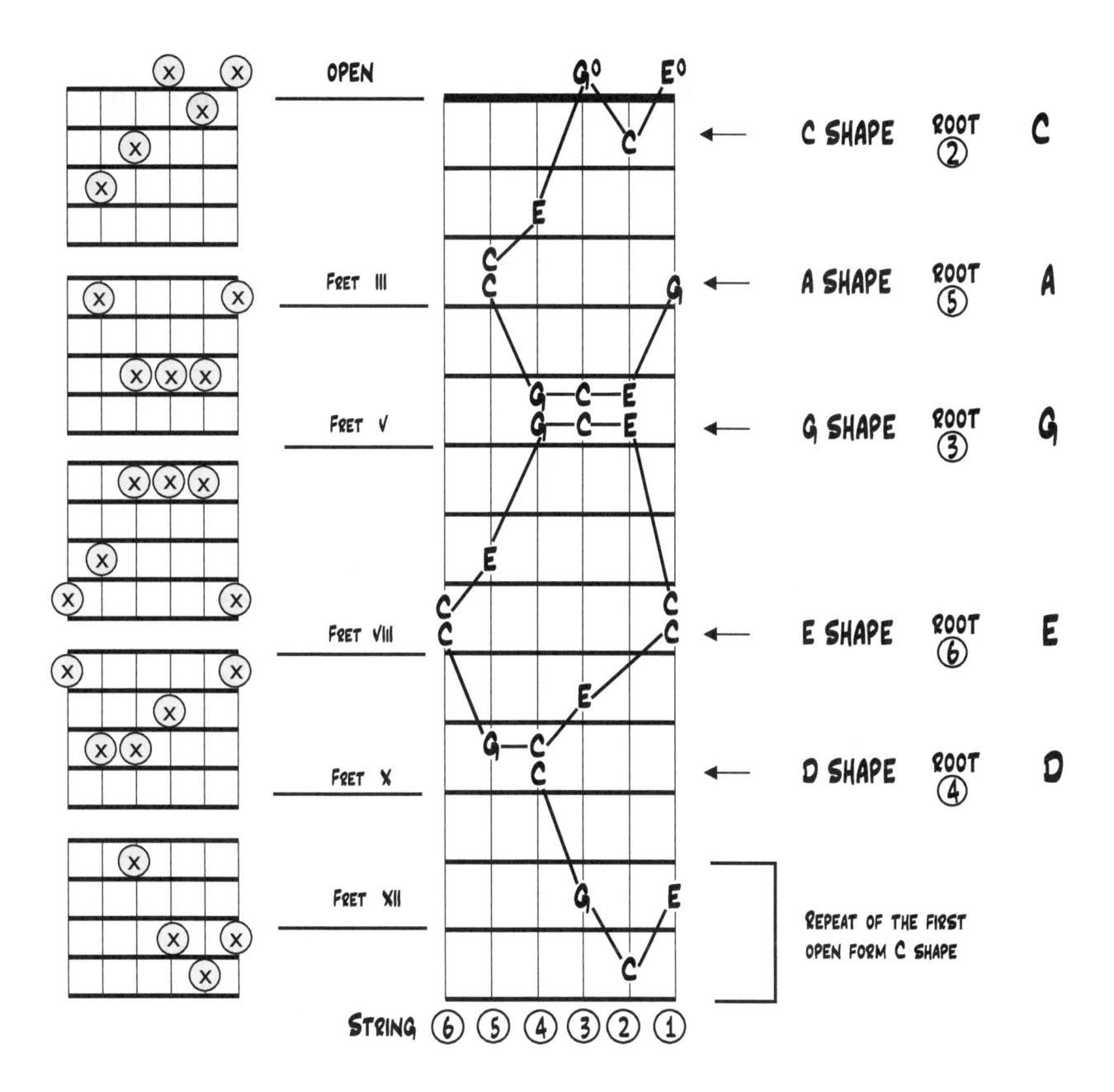

C SHAPE — ROOT ② — C
A SHAPE — ROOT ⑤ — A
G SHAPE — ROOT ③ — G
E SHAPE — ROOT ⑥ — E
D SHAPE — ROOT ④ — D

Repeat of the first open form C shape

String ⑥ ⑤ ④ ③ ② ①

Now try this same logic beginning with A in open position with chords maintaining the same relationships. Then G, then E and finally, D.

From Open Position - C - C A G E D
From Open Position - A - A G E D C
From Open Position - G - G E D C A
From Open Position - E - E D C A G
From Open Position - D - D C A G E

53

VOICE LEADING

Each note in a chord is referred to as a voice. In a chord progression one voice of a chord remains in common or "leads" to the next voice.

Let's examine this in a simple II - V - I progression using common chord voicings.

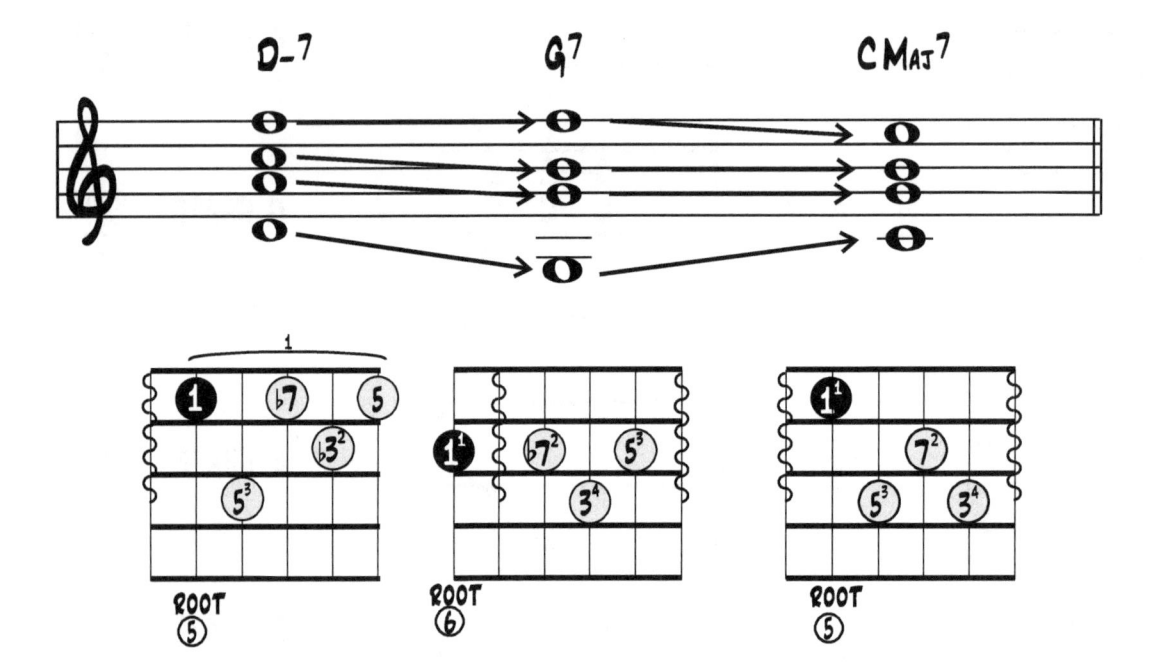

As you can see the F Note in the D-7 is common to the G7 and then falls to the 3rd or E of the C Maj7 chord. Follow the movement of each individual voice and listen.

As a guitar player it is easy to get locked into chord pictures, but remember that chords are made up of individual voices each having their own tendencies toward the next chord.

It will be increasingly important to being to hear the movement of each voice within a chord progression. Think of this as a four voice vocal group with each voice having its own part.

Note also that each of the notes in these chords is derived from the same scale of C major making this progression diatonic (according to the scale).

Now, let's move on to some new chord voicings.

ROOT 4 AND 3 FORMS

It is worth pointing out that the following root 4 and root 3 voicings are no less important than the root 6, 5, 2 voicings.

Make an effort to begin to connect all of the 6, 5, 4, 3 and 2 forms with the same root while thinking of the C A G E D system. The result should be a connection of the entire fretboard with each chord type.

Note how each chord relates to its parent open position chord.

For example:

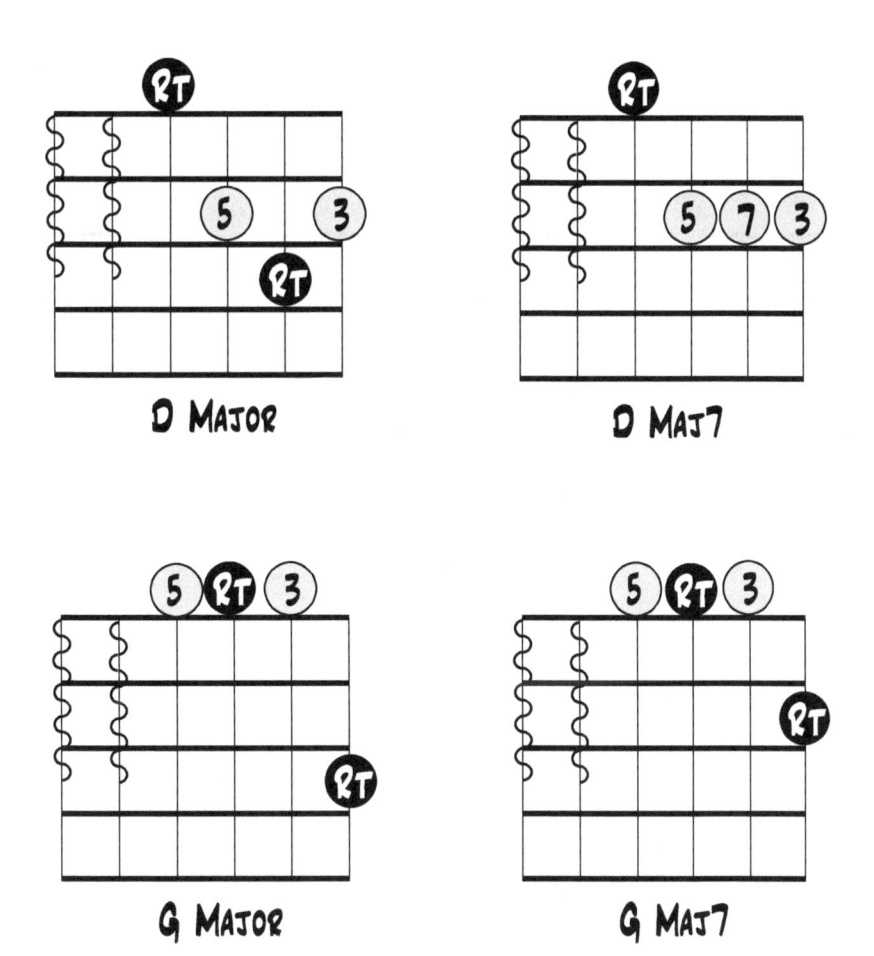

D MAJOR

D MAJ7

G MAJOR

G MAJ7

The chords and arpeggios to follow will NOT suggest fretboard positions. Each chord is presented as a moveable form.

MAJOR 7
ROOT 4, 3

ARPEGGIO

CHORD

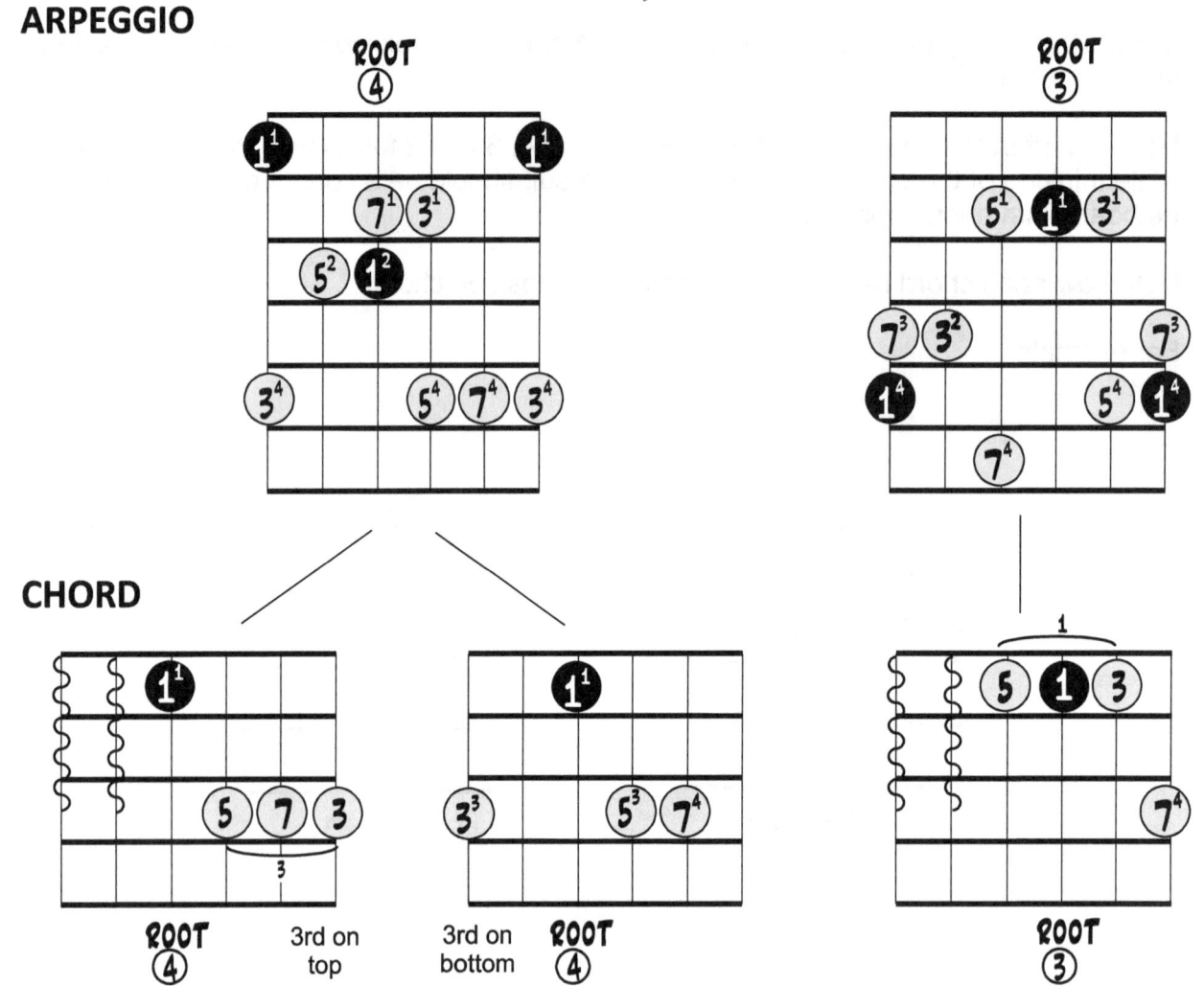

CHORD SPELLING FROM C ROOT

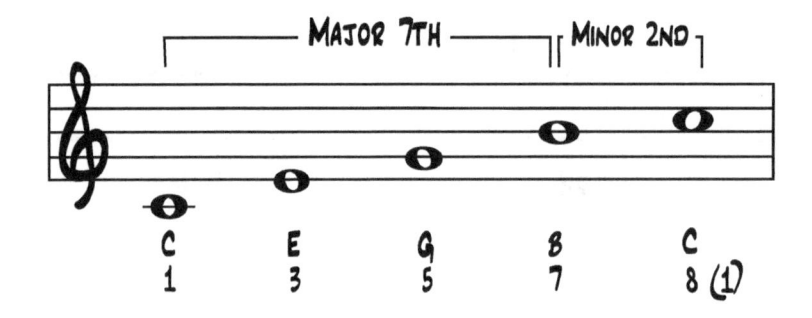

The root 4 voicing produces two very common and useable forms, one with 3rd on top and one with 3rd in the bass. The 3rd in the lowest voice creates a slightly more ambiguous sound but creates nice opportunities for bass lines.

DOMINANT 7
ROOT 4, 3

ARPEGGIO

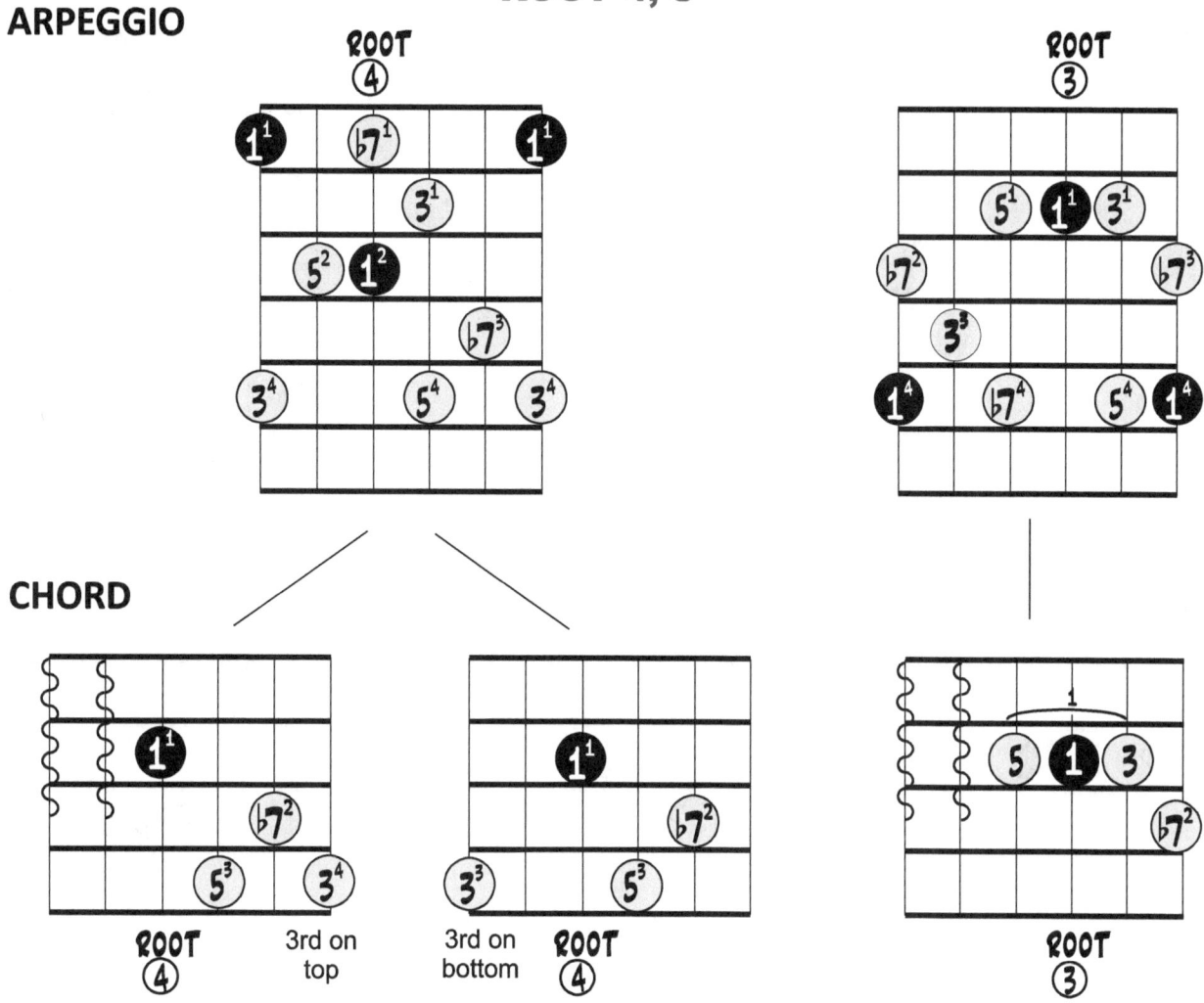

CHORD

3rd on top

3rd on bottom

CHORD SPELLING FROM G ROOT

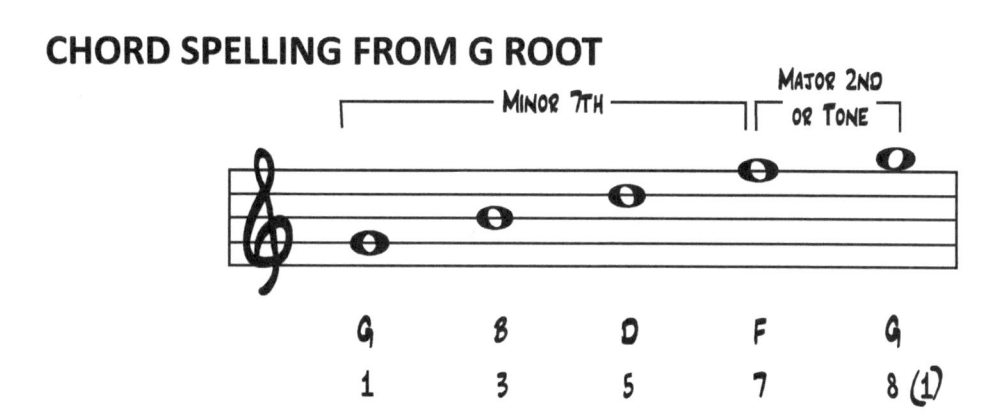

Minor 7th: G, B, D, F
Major 2nd or Tone: F, G

G	B	D	F	G
1	3	5	7	8 (1)

minor 7
ROOT 4, 3

ARPEGGIO

CHORD

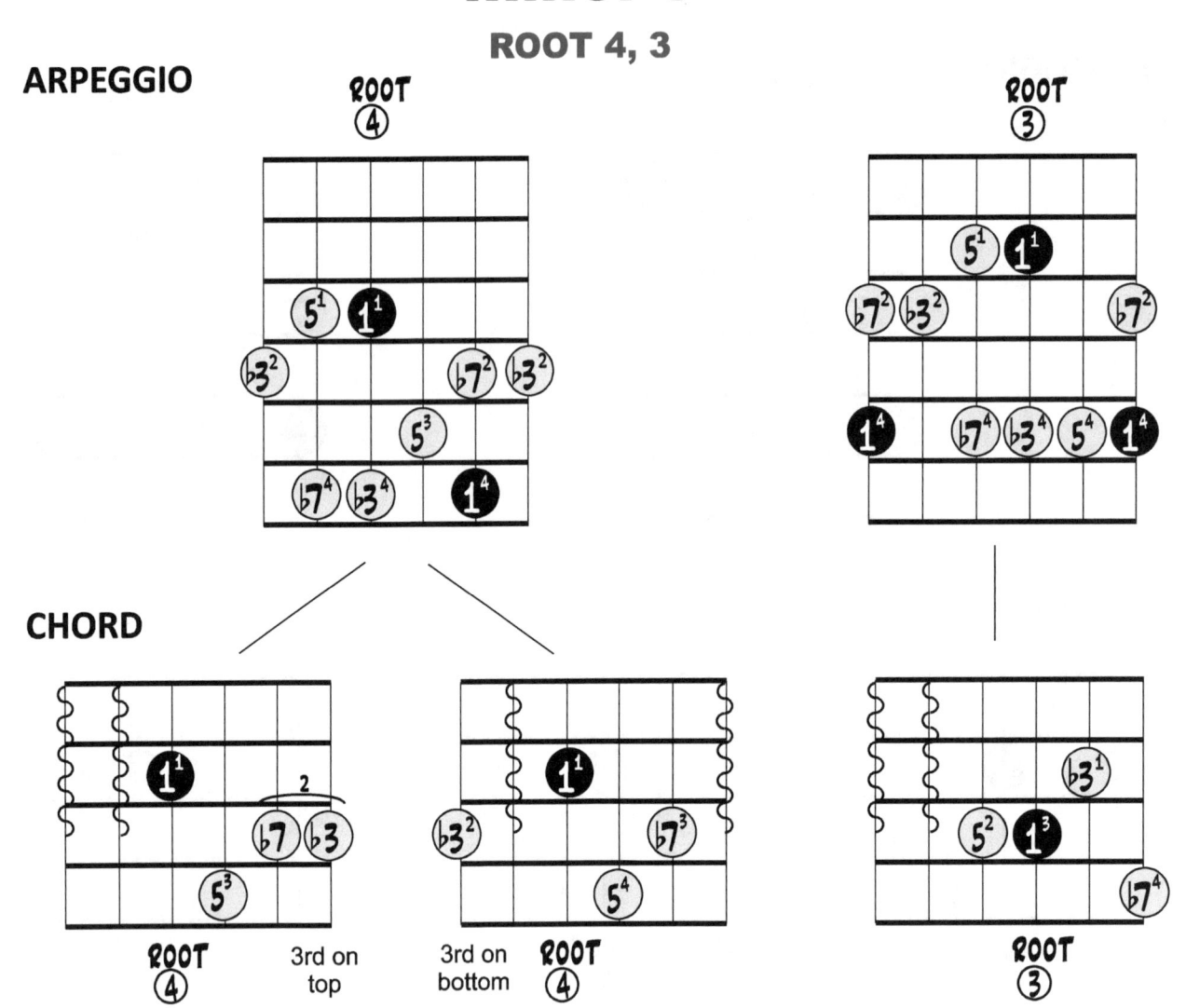

CHORD SPELLING

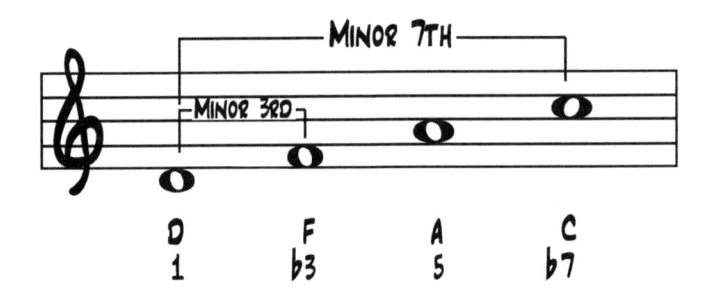

Note that all arpeggio and chord forms are moveable.

minor 7♭5
ROOT 4, 3

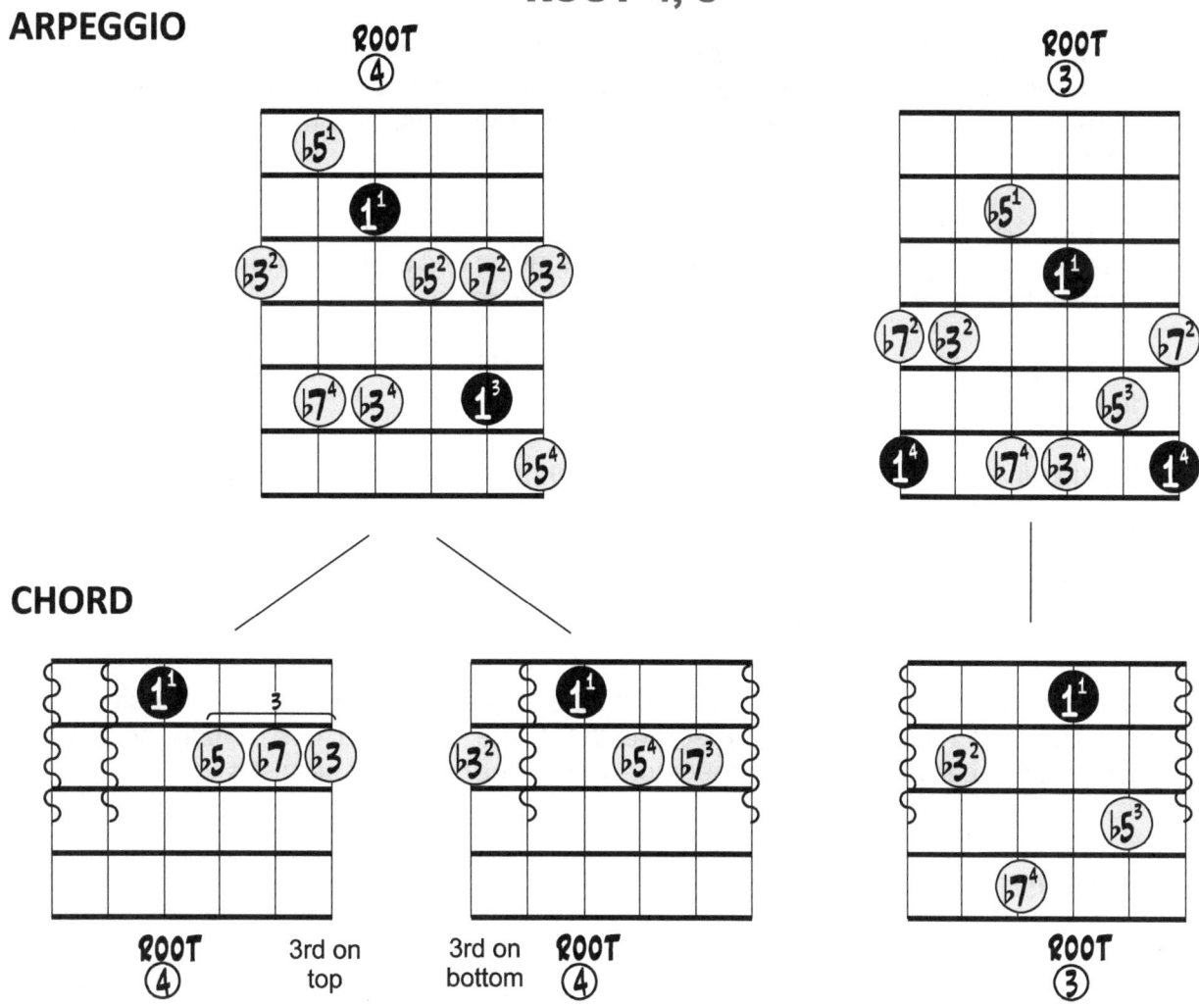

ARPEGGIO

CHORD

CHORD SPELLING

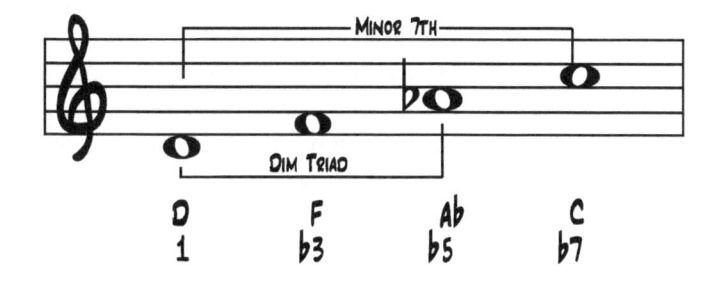

D — 1
F — ♭3
A♭ — ♭5
C — ♭7

Note that the m7♭5 is also referred to as a half diminished and uses this symbol for designation: Ø The m7♭5 is a diminished triad with a minor 7th from the root.

CONNECTING THE FRETBOARD

The fretboard is like a conveyer belt of notes that is divided into scale forms that fit into hand positions. These scales are moveable as are arpeggios and chords. Think of scales as templates for chords and arpeggios, and think of them all as moving together as a group.

On the following pages we revisit the CAGED system to further reveal how all chords and arpeggios fit into this system dovetailing one into the other. For the sake of brevity we have only included the major7, 7 and minor 7 sounds.

Note the relationships to the common open position forms from which these are derived.

To add all of the chord sounds, simply do the necessary alterations to these three types.

Vertical and Horizontal

At this stage the purpose of re-introducing the chords and arpeggios in all positions is to help you visualize and integrate the entire fretboard horizontally so that connections between chords, arpeggios and scales become seamless.

Shifting

When approaching long form arpeggios "across" the fretboard try to always shift on your finger 1 to positions that you have learned vertically without missing any notes of the arpeggios sequence. Try connecting only a couple of adjacent forms at a time and work out your shifts and fingerings carefully, as there are many possibilities.

Arpeggios Practice

Always associate the arpeggio with its related chord form so that you easily recognize the relationships. At the same time think of the chords and arpeggios as "sounds". Above all, listen to, and be able to identify the "sounds" you are learning.

Choose one arpeggio at a time to practice with related chords and do serious repetitions perfectly each time with identical fingerings. Strive for at least 20 at a time, playing slowly and accurately.

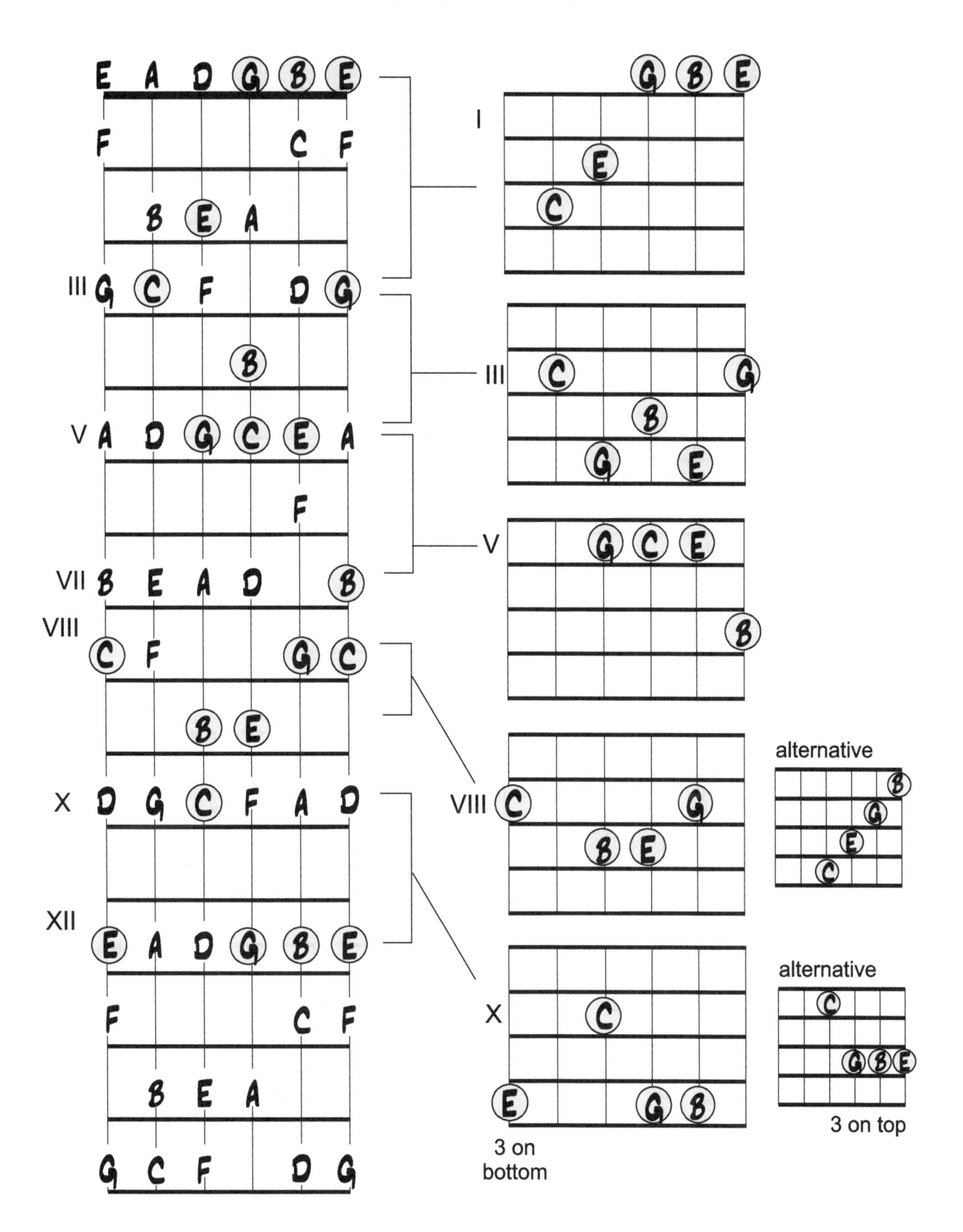

CAGED CONNECTIONS MAJOR 7
(Major Scale)

CAGED CONNECTIONS DOMINANT 7
(Mixolydian Mode)

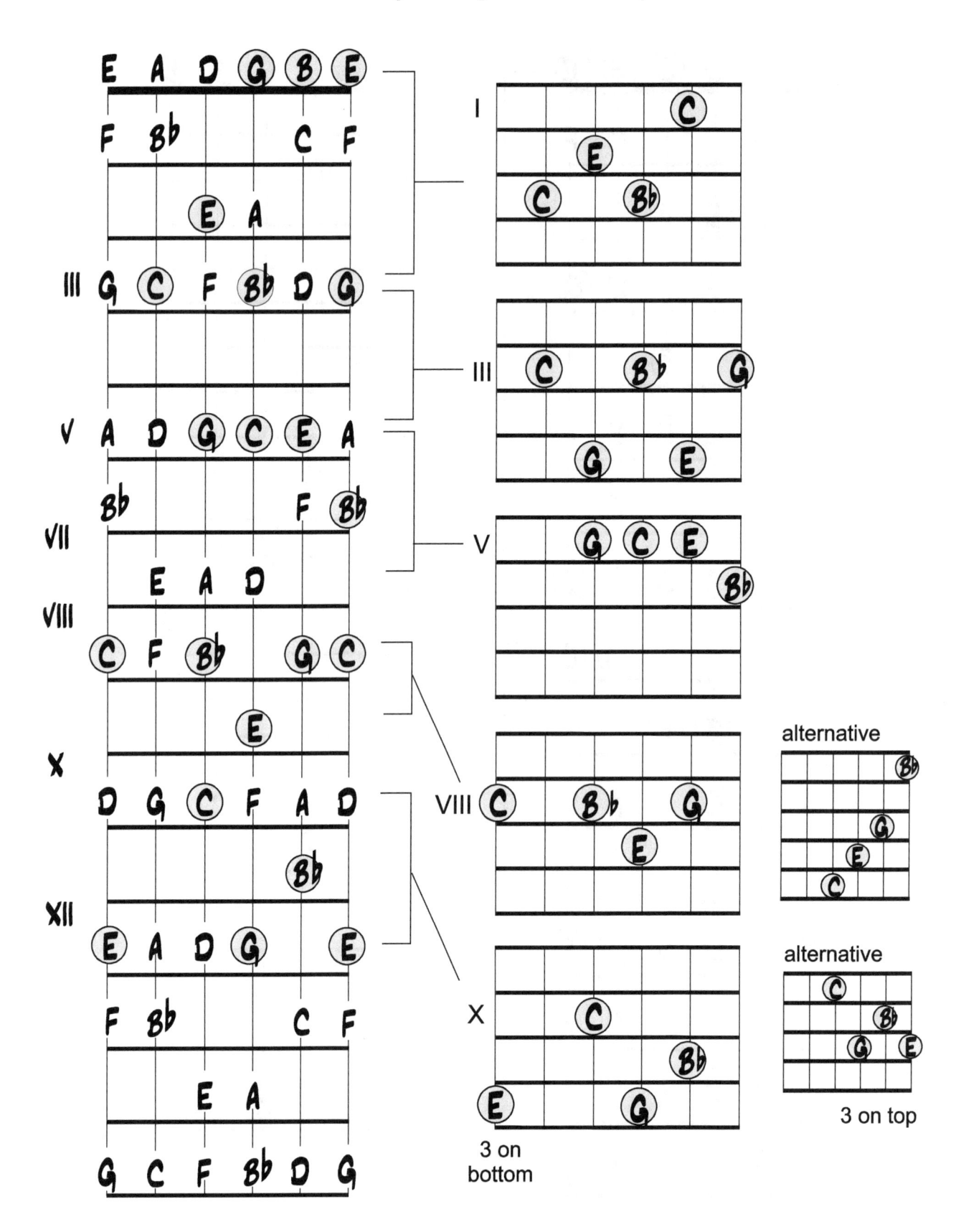

CAGED CONNECTIONS MINOR 7
(Natural Minor)

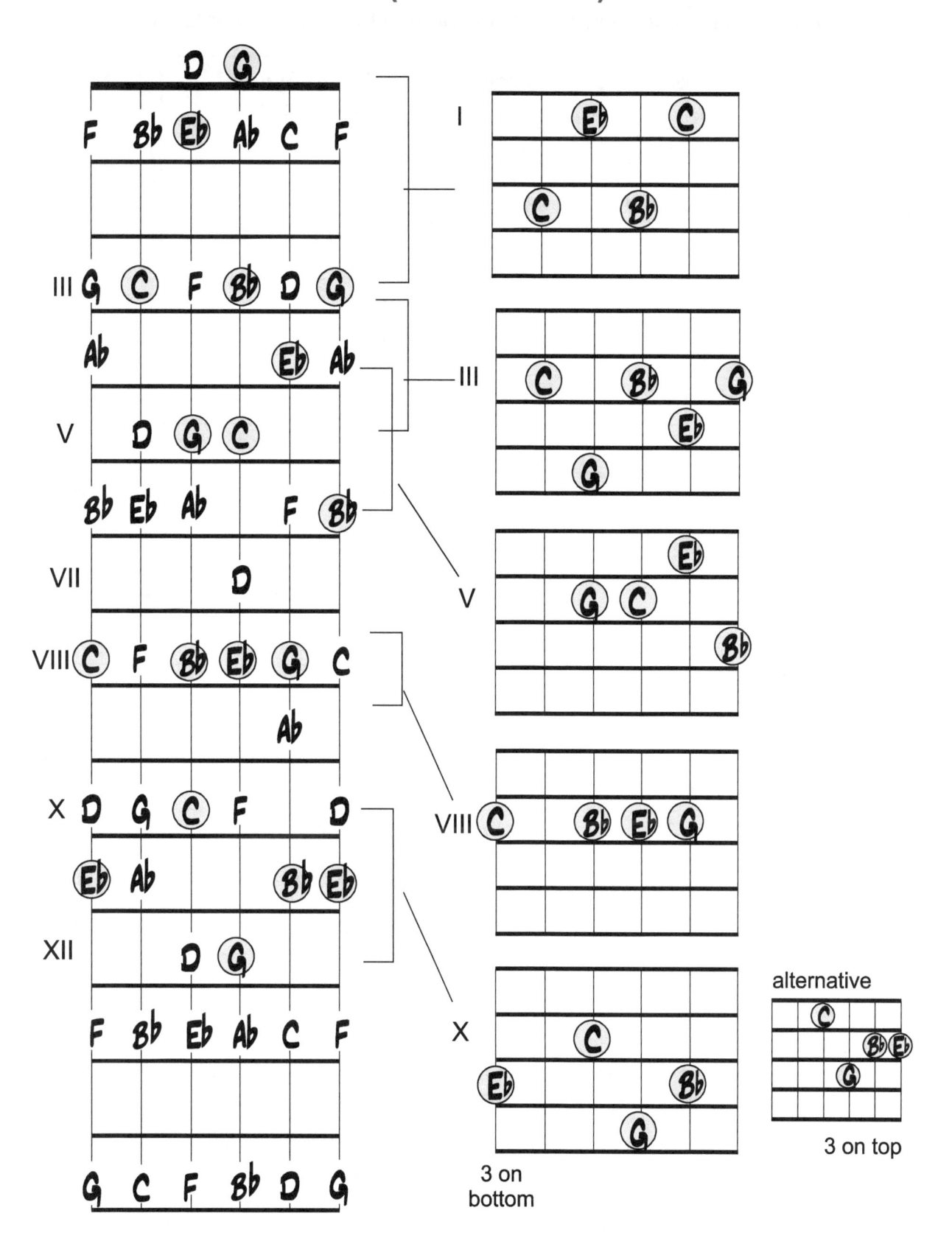

SPELLING INTERVALS AND CHORDS
PARALLEL TONAL CENTRE

The following chords are spelled in Parallel or from the same root or tonal centre.

Root Triad	Chord Type	Formula	Chord Symbol (from root C)	Notes
Major	Major Triad	1 3 5	C	C E G
Minor	Minor Triad	1 ♭3 5	Cm	C E♭ G
Diminished	Diminished	1 ♭3 ♭5	Cdim	C E♭ G♭
Augmented	Augmented	1 3 #5	Caug	C E G#
Major	Major 6	1 3 5 6	C Maj6	C E G A
Major	Major 6/9	1 3 5 6 9	C Maj6/9	C E G A D
Minor	Minor 6	1 ♭3 5 6	Cm6	C E♭ G A
Major	Major 7	1 3 5 7	C Maj7	C E G B
Major	Dominant 7	1 3 5 ♭7	C7	C E G B♭
Major	Major 9	1 3 5 7 9	C Maj9	C E G B D
Augmented	Dominant 7#5	1 3 #5 ♭7	C7#5, C7aug, C7+	C E G# B♭
Diminished	Dominant 7♭5	1 3 ♭5 ♭7	C7♭5	C E G♭ B♭
Major	Dominant 7#9	1 3 5 ♭7 #9	C7#9	C E G B♭ D#
Major	Dominant 7♭9	1 3 5 7♭9	C7♭9	C E G B♭ D♭
Minor	Minor 7	1 ♭3 5 ♭7	Cm7, Cmin7, C-7	C E♭ G B♭
Diminished	Minor 7♭5	1 ♭3 ♭5 ♭7	Cm7♭5, C half-dim, CØ	C E♭ G♭ B♭
Minor	Minor Major 7	1 ♭3 5 7	CmMaj7, Cm#7	C E♭ G B
Diminished	Diminished 7	1 ♭3 ♭5 ♭♭7	Cdim7, C°7	C E♭ G♭ B♭♭
Minor	Minor 9	1 ♭3 5 ♭7 9	Cm9	C E♭ G B♭ D

The chords above are indicated with a root triad for reference. A chord sound is largely a product of its voicing. The word "voicing" refers to how the notes in a chord are arranged.

Chords sometimes use enharmonic equivalents. For example, the diminished 7th chord uses a double flat 7 (♭♭7) or diminished 7th from the root, the harmonic equivalent to a 6th.

The above chart is not a complete representation of possibilities but serves as a good starting point. Remember that 5ths and roots of chords are often eliminated.

CHORD VOICINGS GLOSSARY

The following chord voicing glossary is by no means exhaustive, but instead reflects some of the most common and practical forms.

Each of the groups is divided into categories of string roots AND major, minor and dominant sounds. These "sounds" will translate directly to the common chord progressions.

Learn these voicings within the context of chord progressions, the II - V - I is a good place to start. Use the diminished forms to connect the I - I chromatically to start. Then, I suggest moving on to some simple standards.

Try adding one new chord at a time to your repertoire and get it under your fingers with lots of slow repetition.

Make sure you are able to play the underlying scale form of each chord. Capture the sound of the chord within the scale sound.

For example:

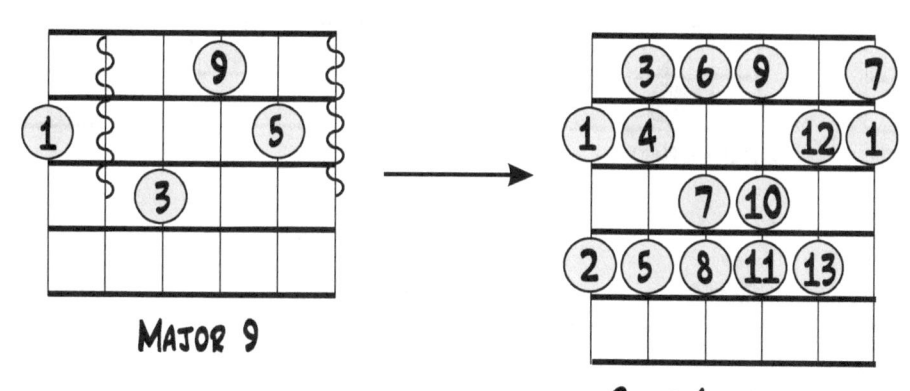

MAJOR 9 → ROOT 6 MAJOR SCALE
NOTE POSITIONS OF CHORD TONES

And another:

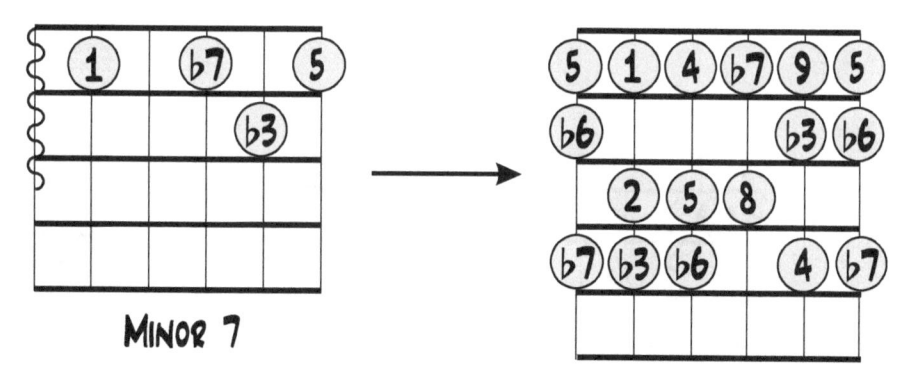

MINOR 7 → ROOT 5 NATURAL MINOR SCALE

CHORD VOICING GLOSSARY

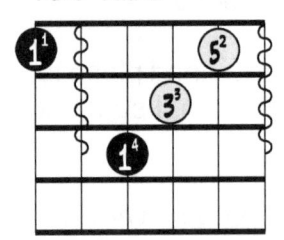

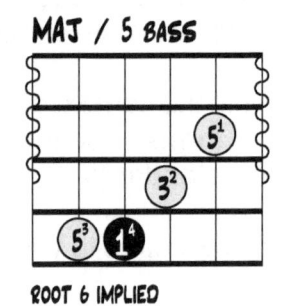

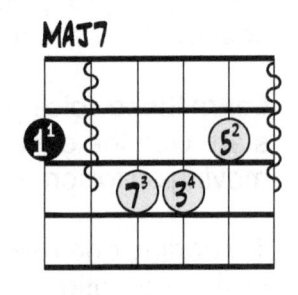

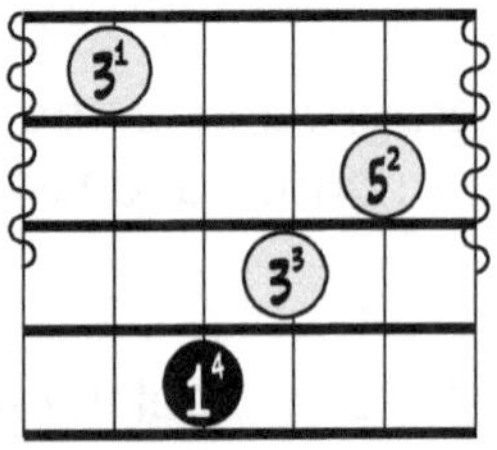

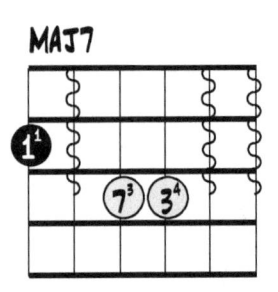

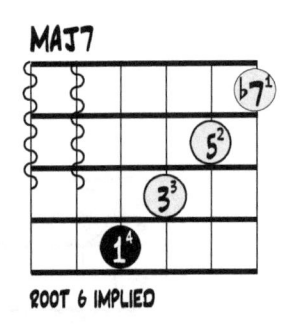

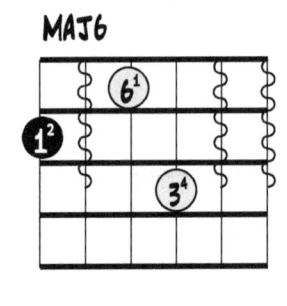

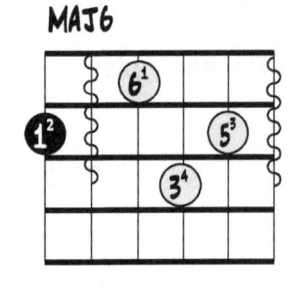

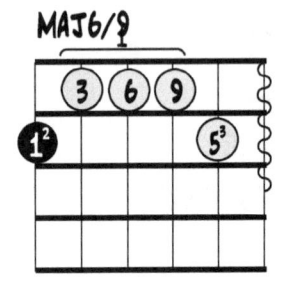

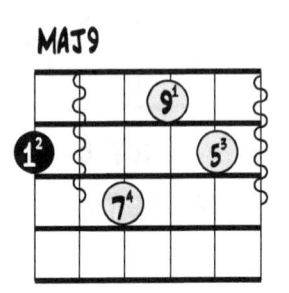

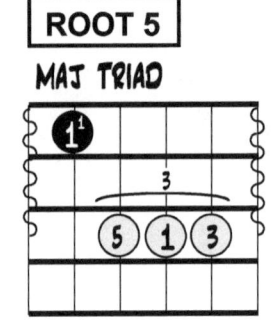

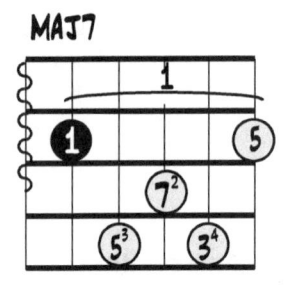

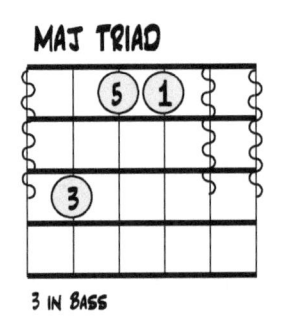

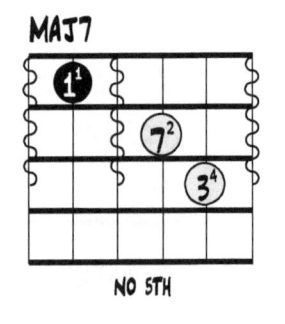

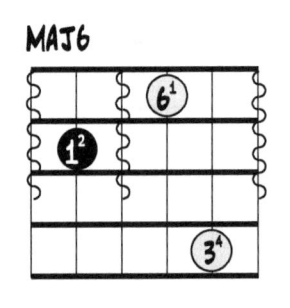

MAJOR

ROOT 6

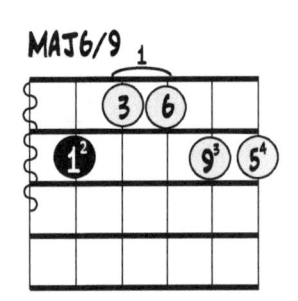

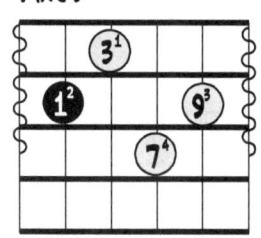

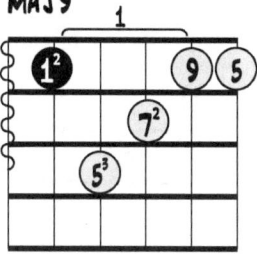

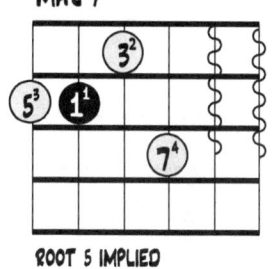

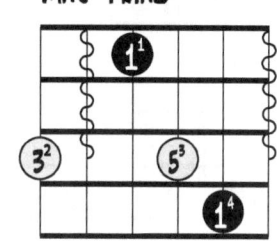

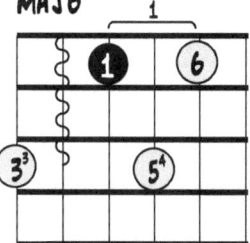

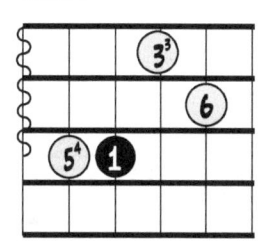

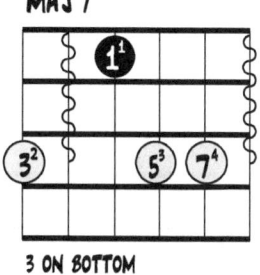

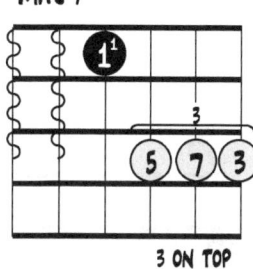

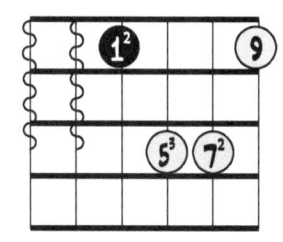

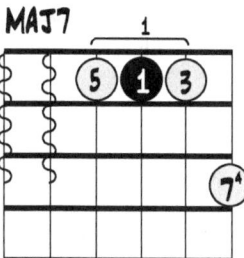

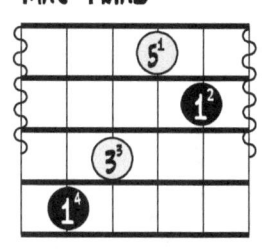

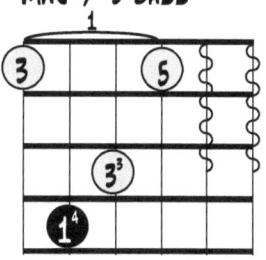

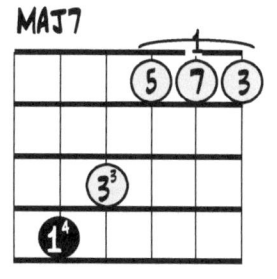

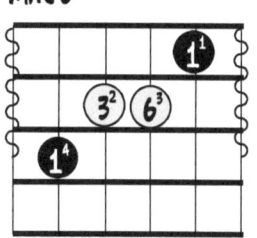

MAJOR

DOMINANT

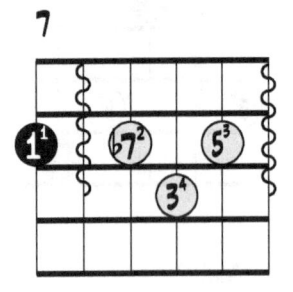

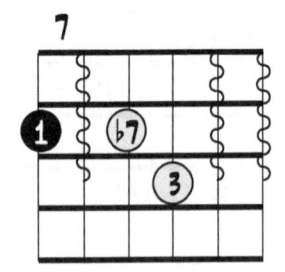

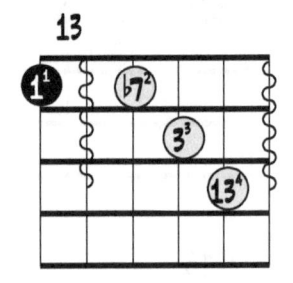

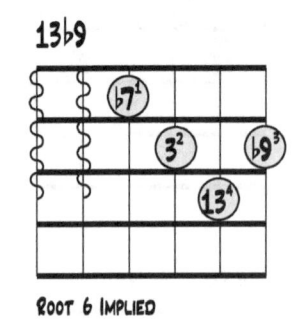

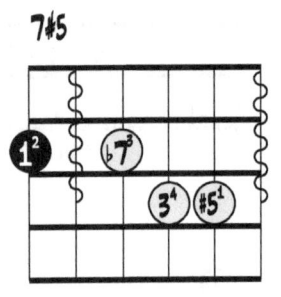

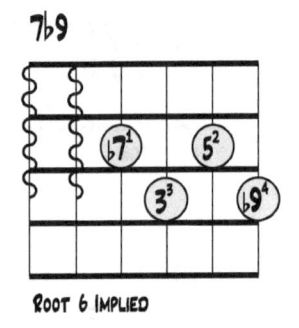

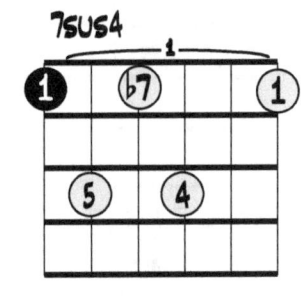

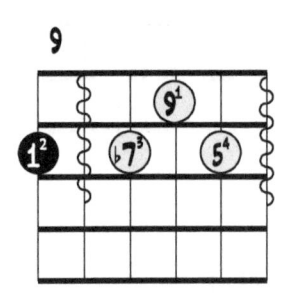

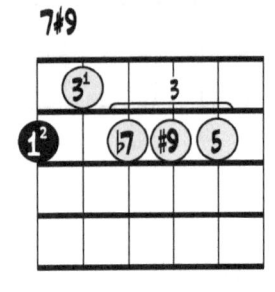

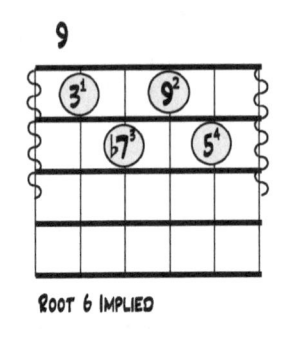

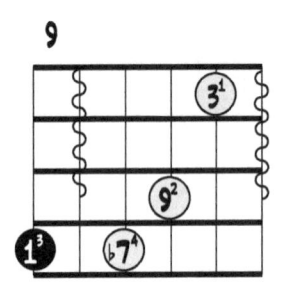

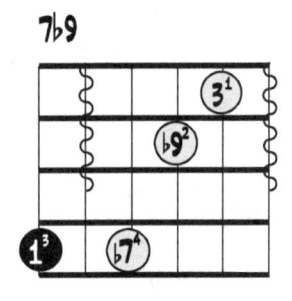

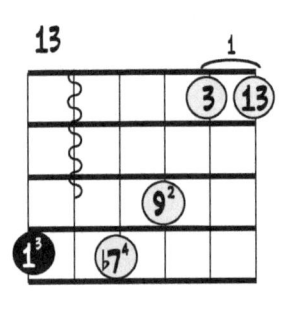

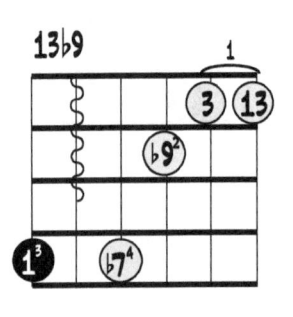

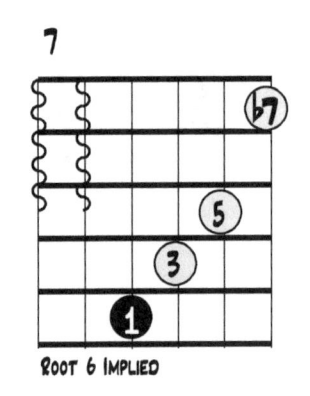

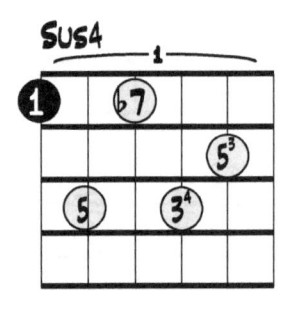

ROOT 6

DOMINANT

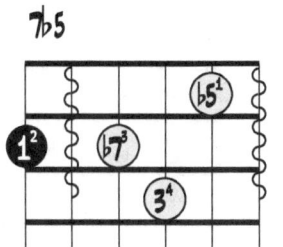

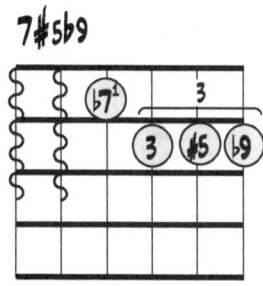

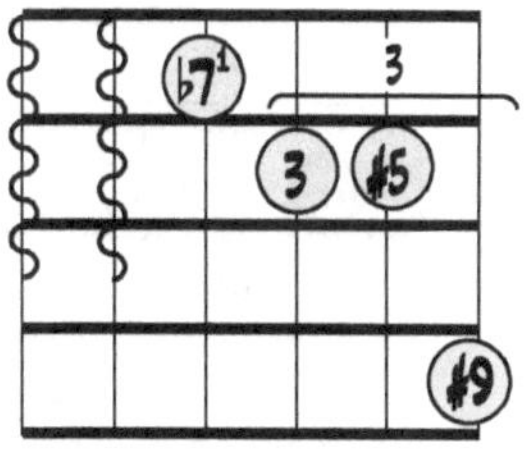

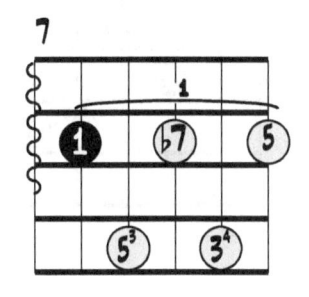

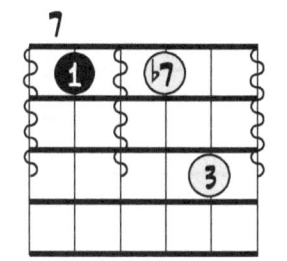

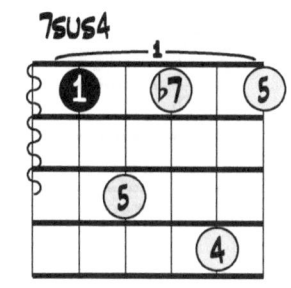

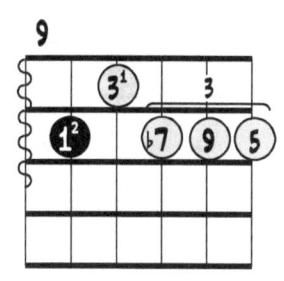

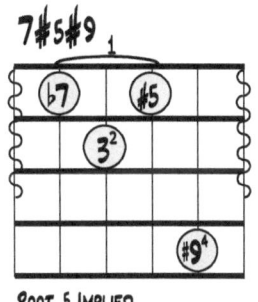

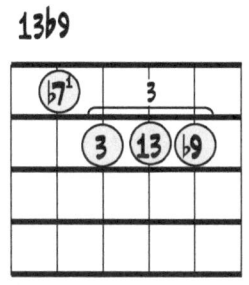

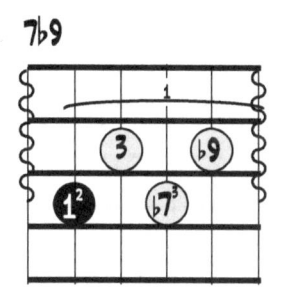

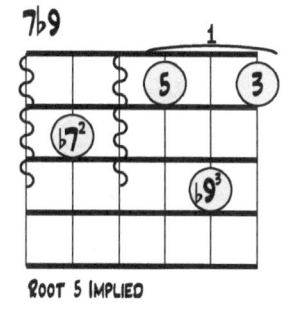

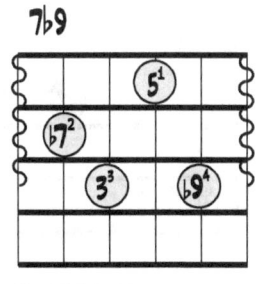

ROOT 6

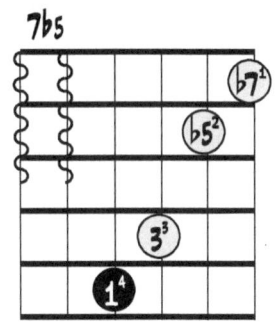

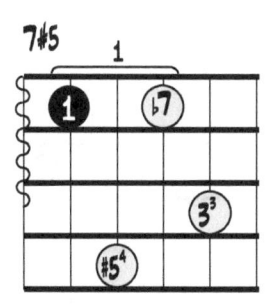

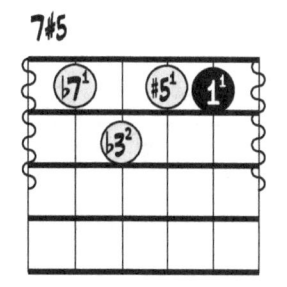

ROOT 5

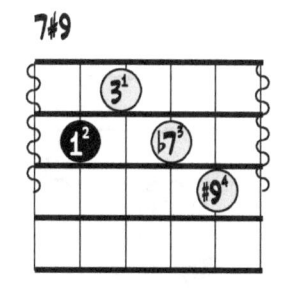

DOMINANT

ROOT 5

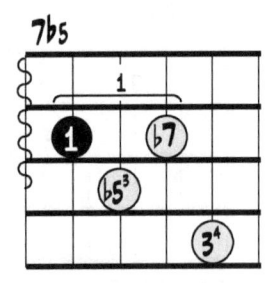

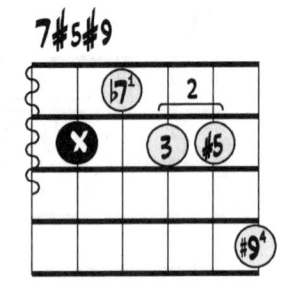

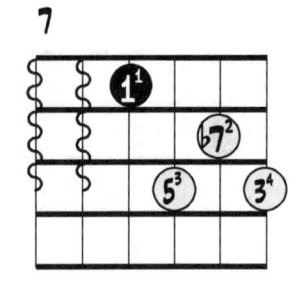

7b5 | 7#5#9 | 7

ROOT 4

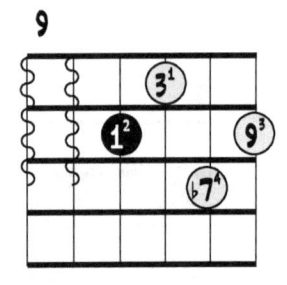

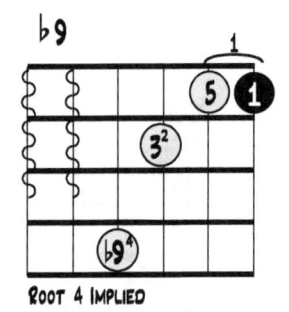

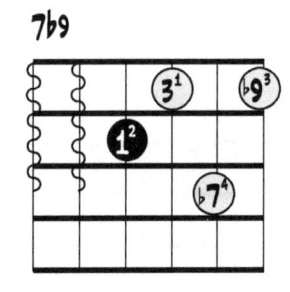

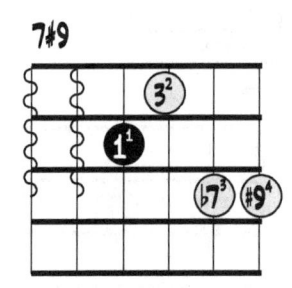

9 | b9 (Root 4 implied) | 7b9 | 7#9

ROOT 3

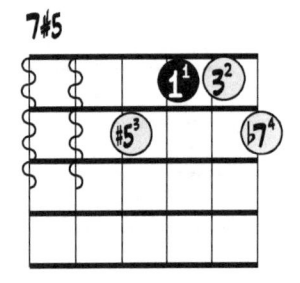

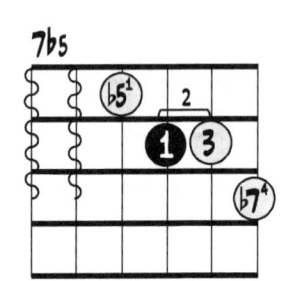

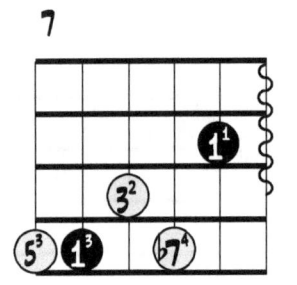

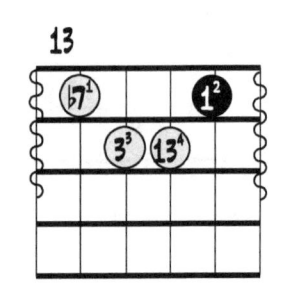

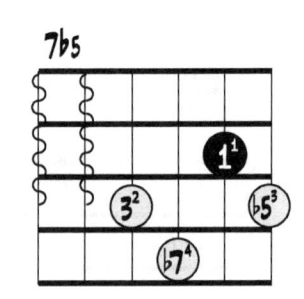

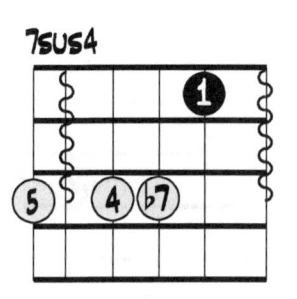

7#5 | 7b5

ROOT 2

7 | 13 | 7b5 | 7sus4

70

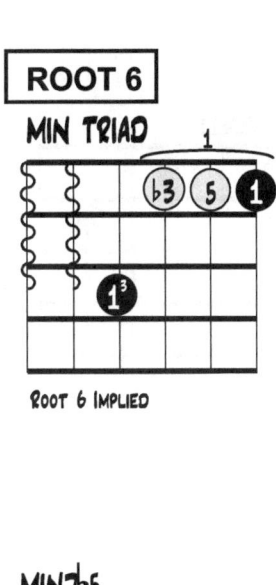

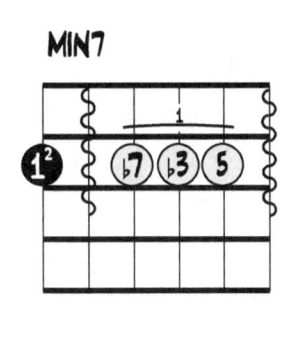

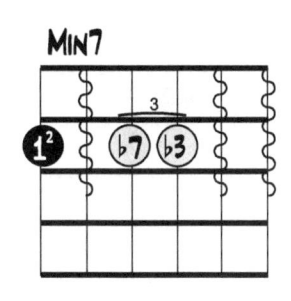

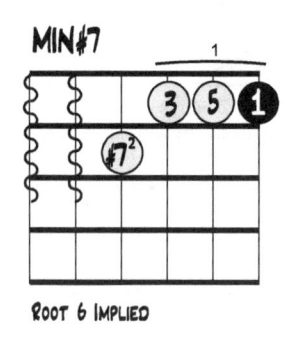

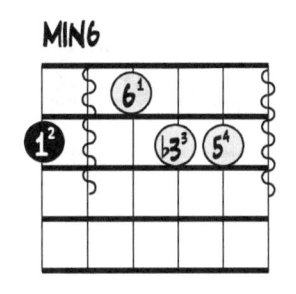

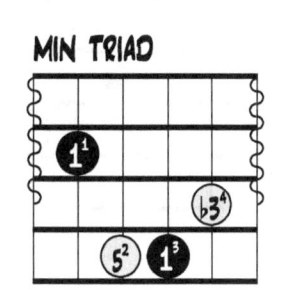

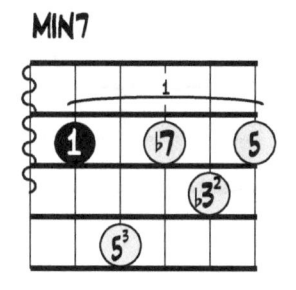

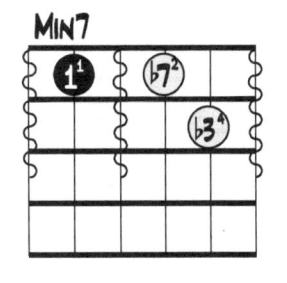

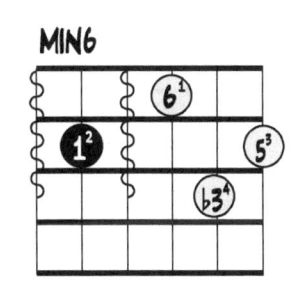

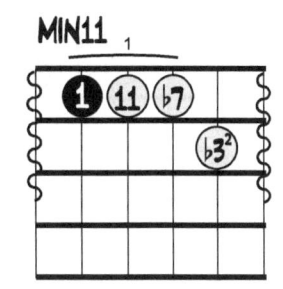

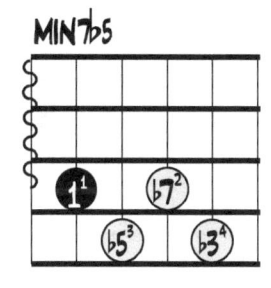

MINOR

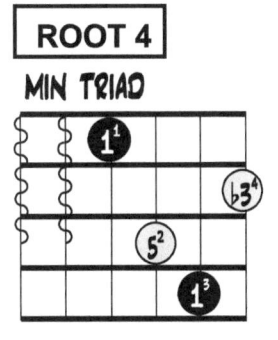

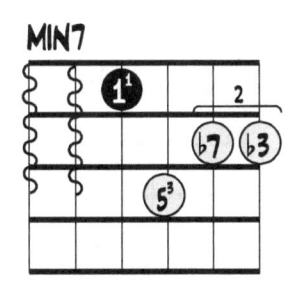

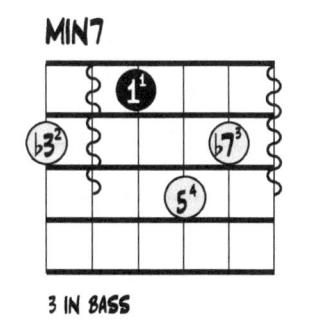

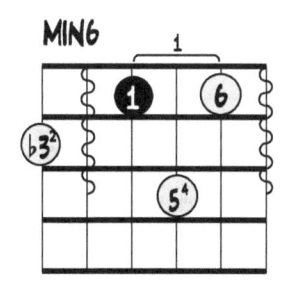

MINOR

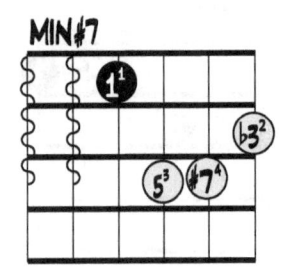

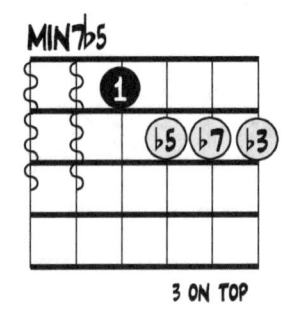

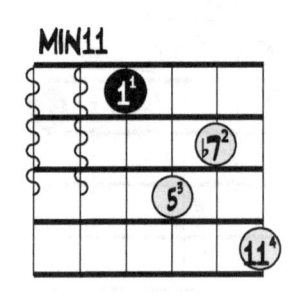

ROOT 4

MIN♯7 — 1, ♭3, 5, ♯7

MIN7♭5 — 1, ♭3, ♭5, ♭7 (3 lowest voice)

MIN7♭5 — 1, ♭5, ♭7, ♭3 (3 on top)

MIN11 — 1, ♭7, 5, 11

ROOT 3

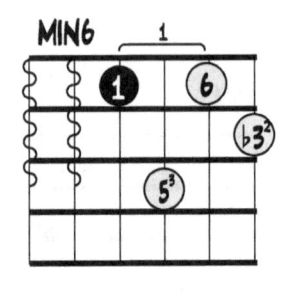

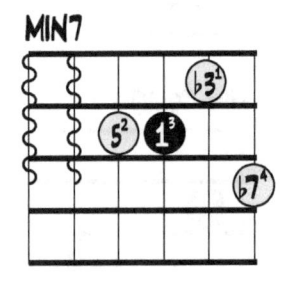

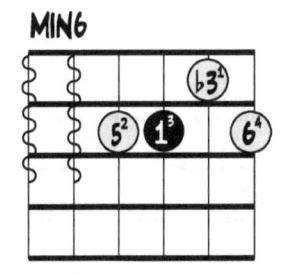

MIN6 — 1, 6, ♭3, 5

MIN7 — ♭3, 5, 1, ♭7

MIN6 — ♭3, 5, 1, 6

ROOT 2

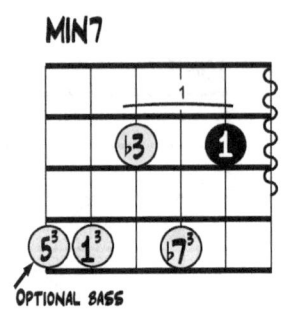

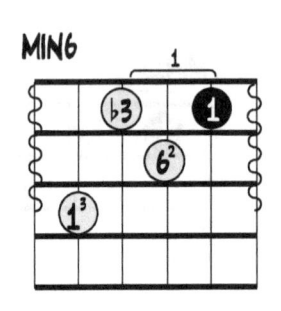

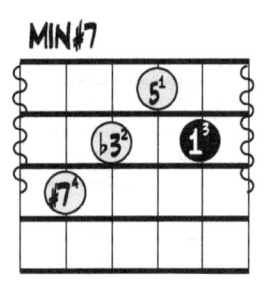

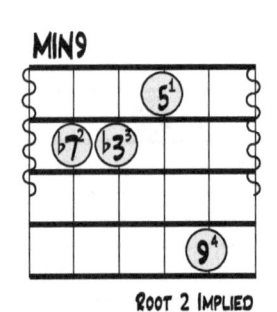

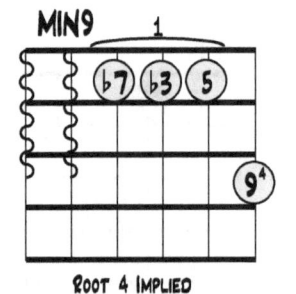

MIN7 — ♭3, 1, (5, 1, ♭7 optional bass)

MIN6 — ♭3, 1, 6, 1

MIN TRIAD — 5, ♭3, 1, 1

MIN♯7 — 5, ♭3, 1, ♯7

MIN7♭5 — ♭5, ♭7, ♭3, 1 (Note ♭7 in the lowest voice)

MIN9 — 5, ♭7, ♭3, 9 (Root 2 implied)

MIN9 — ♭7, ♭3, 5, 9 (Root 4 implied)

72

DIMINISHED (Dominant)

NOTE: In a diminished chord every note can be a root note. Fingerings only marked.

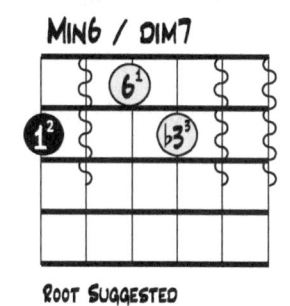

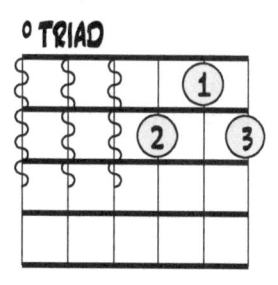

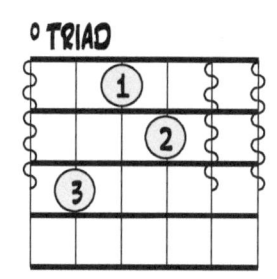

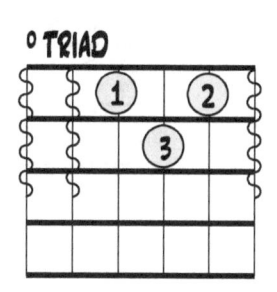

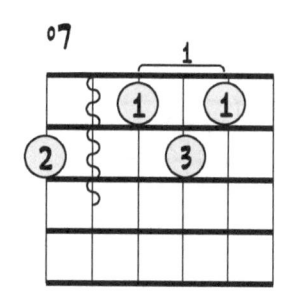

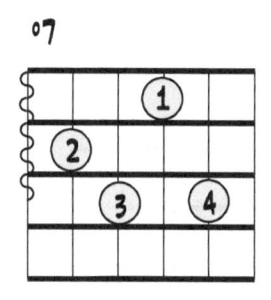

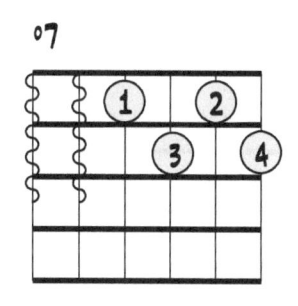

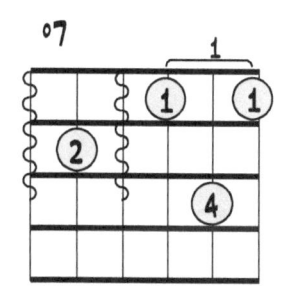

ENHARMONIC EQUIVALENTS

The same chord shape can often have different names by simply moving the root. These new chords will have different functions and sounds depending on musical context. The root of the chord will move to a different position and the other chord tones will fall into relationship with the new root position.

In other words the "shape and fingering" of the chord will not change, only the chord name and its function..

Let's take a look at two chord examples to demonstrate this:

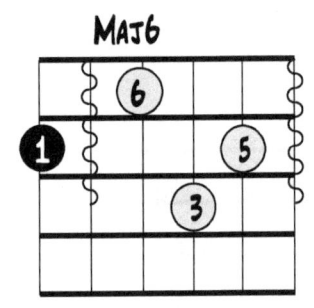

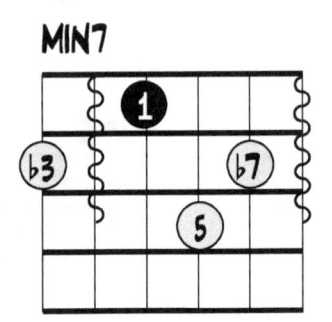

MAJ6

MIN7

Three-note chords can be even more harmonically ambiguous especially when the root is implied as:

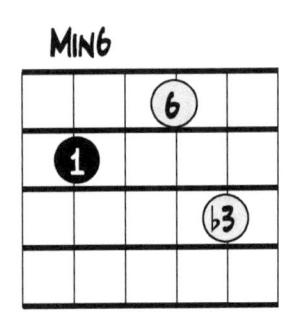

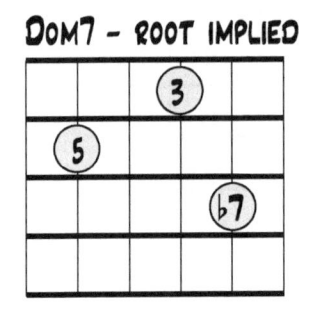

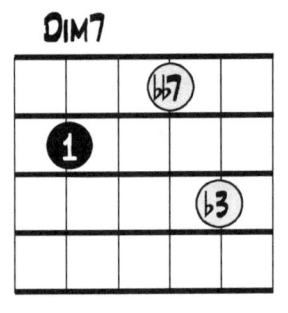

MIN6

DOM7 - ROOT IMPLIED

DIM7

There are many other examples of enharmonic equivilents too numerous for the scope of this book. Consider and examine your own chord voicings by using the same chord shapes and rearranging the chord tones to create different chord names using the same fingerings. Dominant 7ths, and diminished and minor 6ths are especially revealing.

A SHORT HISTORY OF THE RHYTHM CHORD

Each of the arpeggios in this book are associated with their related rhythm chord voicings as illustrated thus providing not only arpeggio forms but a series of useful related rhythm chord voicings as well. For this reason I thought it might be worth explaining why these specific chord voicings were chosen and why these chords are referred to as "rhythm chords".

Rhythm chords or "Jazz" rhythm chords have strong defining musical characteristics as well as a rather colorful history. The guitar has always had an intimate relationship with dance and thus rhythm and accompaniment in a host of different styles. For example the Flamenco guitar's dance origins go back to the 18th century. In this Spanish folk art form the guitar is used as the driving rhythmic force behind the dance, the design of the instrument as well as the playing technique are in fact defined by this. This percussive playing style is deeply rooted in the Gypsy folk music tradition which is expressed in the Jazz Manouche or Gypsy Jazz tradition. In fact Django Rheinhardt was of the same Romani or Spanish descent as many of the great Flamenco artists. This percussive rhythmic playing style eventually became an intrinsic part of the overall modern Jazz guitar sound.

The beginning of the 20th century saw the guitar as the chosen instrument of Cowboys, Blues and Folk musicians but over a few short years the creative genius of a new generation with amplifiers began to redefine the instrument. This new technological marvel of amplification added an entirely new dimension to the instrument that led to it becoming a strong voice that could be heard even over horn sections. This began to reveal the true harmonic capabilities and complexities of the instrument. Now large audiences could hear the subtleties of the guitar's harmonies as if they were sitting beside the performers.

By the late 30s players like Charlie Christian, Carl Kress, George Barnes were now taking solos and the banjo (still being used by Duke Ellington in his orchestra) was increasingly being replaced by the sounds of the F Hole Arch top electric jazz guitar. The once intimate and delicate and soft spoken portable parlour instrument had with the event of the amp and pickup become as dynamic as its cumbersome mechanical cousin, the piano. Not only was the guitar becoming the driving harmonic pulse behind a host of big bands but it was also increasingly being recognized as a small ensemble and solo instrument which of course led to the late 50's and beyond.

Throughout this musical and guitaristic development guitarists chose chord voicings for their ability to be changed quickly in any key in order to drive out a steady rhythm and be heard within the rhythm section. The chords had to have a balanced sound without the unnecessary duplication of notes within the chords and generally without open strings . Over the years many players settled on a group of the same chord voicings because of their ease of use and functionality and these were eventually referred to simply as "rhythm chords" or often colloquially as "Jazz chords".

Due to their harmonic economy, ease of use and musicality these same chords have been passed down and to this day are considered an essential part of every guitarist's vocabulary. These tried and true forms are used by College level guitar programs all over North America to introduce developing players to reading changes and playing chord charts much in the same way they were originally used by the Jazz guitar greats.

In the arpeggios book we are using many of these same voicings simply because of the popularity they have enjoyed for a century or so and because they just work and sound great. There are other voicings that could be effective as well but for the purposes of this book we have carefully chosen some of the most useful and universal.

Other great players to listen to who were influenced by the great swing era and who in turn came to influence entire generations of new players are: Joe Pass, Herb Ellis, Barney Kessell, Grant Green, Wes Montgomery, Kenny Burrell, Tal Farlow, Lenny Breau, Howard Roberts, Les Paul.

HISTORY OF THE REAL FAKE BOOK

There was a time not long ago when in order to get a fake book full of great standard tunes you had to go to your local music store and ask for an under-the-counter illegal copy. The 4 or 5 hundred page handwritten and then mechanically copied book would then be handed off in an under-the-table cash transaction and you would leave in musical anticipation, contraband in hand.

This clandestine interchange was a necessity because the original editions of the Real Book were written without the necessary copyrights. This legal requirement was sacrificed in favour of creating an accurate central reference point for the great jazz standards that would be enjoyed by generations of musicians who could now share accurace lead sheets.

The story goes that the "Real Book" had been written and compiled by students at Berklee College, but of course the original transcribers weren't quick to pen their names on illegally copied intellectual property.

This book, through its underground distribution channels ultimately went through five editions and fell into the hands of amateur and professional musicians from New York to Vancouver, before the Hal Leonard Corporation purchased the majority of the copyrights in 2004 and subsequently released the first legit version, the sixth edition. Despite the fact that many of the song in the original version were missing, the now legal version could now be found in the print music section of music stores.

The fundamental elements of every song are melody, harmony, form and time. The real Fake Book format provides a foundation for these elements in a simple and easy-to-read format that is designed to be read without turning pages. Thus, making it an ideal companion for the gigging musician.

MASTER FRETBOARD

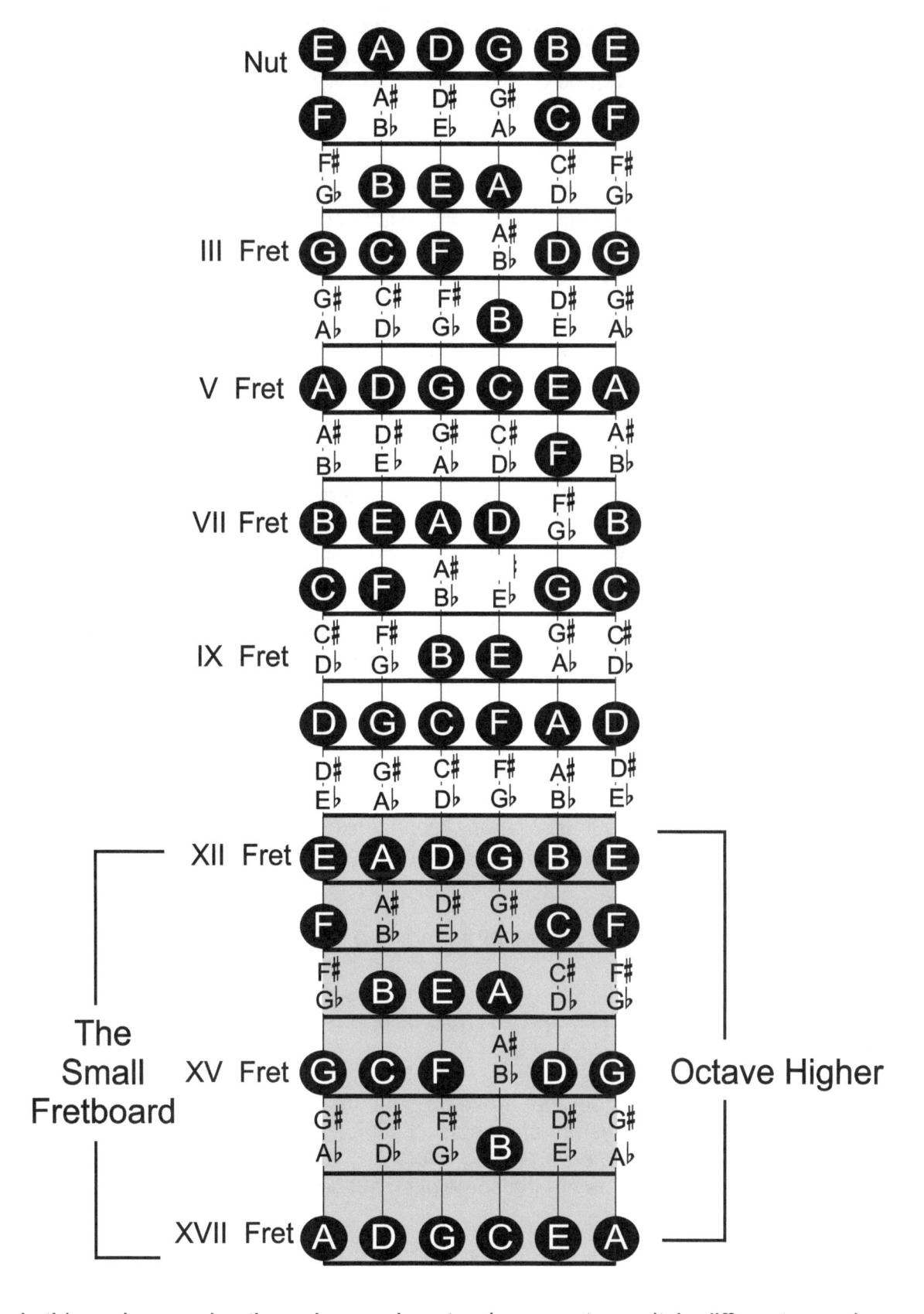

Nut	E	A	D	G	B	E
	F	A#/Bb	D#/Eb	G#/Ab	C	F
	F#/Gb	B	E	A	C#/Db	F#/Gb
III Fret	G	C	F	A#/Bb	D	G
	G#/Ab	C#/Db	F#/Gb	B	D#/Eb	G#/Ab
V Fret	A	D	G	C	E	A
	A#/Bb	D#/Eb	G#/Ab	C#/Db	F	A#/Bb
VII Fret	B	E	A	D	F#/Gb	B
	C	F	A#/Bb	D#/Eb	G	C
IX Fret	C#/Db	F#/Gb	B	E	G#/Ab	C#/Db
	D	G	C	F	A	D
	D#/Eb	G#/Ab	C#/Db	F#/Gb	A#/Bb	D#/Eb
XII Fret	E	A	D	G	B	E
	F	A#/Bb	D#/Eb	G#/Ab	C	F
	F#/Gb	B	E	A	C#/Db	F#/Gb
XV Fret	G	C	F	A#/Bb	D	G
	G#/Ab	C#/Db	F#/Gb	B	D#/Eb	G#/Ab
XVII Fret	A	D	G	C	E	A

The Small Fretboard — **Octave Higher**

Study this and memorize the enharmonic notes (same note or pitch, different name).

GLOSSARY OF TERMS

Accidental - a sharp, flat or natural sign written into the body of a piece of music.

Allegro - indicates a fast tempo.

Andante - indicates a medium tempo.

Arpeggio - often referred to as a broken chord, the notes of a chord played in a linear or melodic sequence and sounded individually. A linear or melodic expression of harmony.

Ascending - moving higher in pitch.

Augmented Chord - a triad with two consecutive major 3rds thus producing a sharp 5 at the 5th of the chord. Augmented 7th chords have an augmented triad and include the mixolydian or lowered 7th. This chord is written as 7#5.

Bar Line - the line that separates measures or bars.

Beat - beat or pulse, the implied and intrinsic foundation of rhythm.

BPM - beats per minute, the speed or tempo at which a piece of music is played that is often expressed as a metronome marking ex. ♩ = 40

Chord - 2 or more notes sounded simultaneously, chords can be played by polyphonic instruments such as piano and guitar but not by monophonic instruments.

Chord Chart - a progression of chords shown with bar lines and sections and often with a tempo indication but without the melody.

Chord Scale - the notes in a scale arranged into a chord and then that chord voicing moves by scale steps throughout the given scale while remaining in the fixed intervallic relationships or specific inversion of that chord. For example 1st inversion triads through the scale of C major.

Chord Spelling - the letter names of the notes of a chord as derived from their parent scale.

Chord Tone - A note that belongs to a chord as opposed to a scale tone which may or may not be part of a chord.

Chromatic Scale - the scale that moves by the smallest increments of a semitone and uses all 12 notes in our system of music including the natural notes and the sharps and flats. It would be the same as playing every key on the piano in succession. (Notes separated by a diagonal line are the same pitch but have a different name, they are called enharmonic)

$$A - A\sharp/B\flat - B - C - C\sharp/D\flat - D - D\sharp/E\flat - E - F - F\sharp/G\flat - G - G\sharp/A\flat - A$$

Accidental - a sharp, flat or natural sign written into the body of a piece of music.

Allegro - indicates a fast tempo.

Andante - indicates a medium tempo.

Arpeggio - often referred to as a broken chord, the notes of a chord played in a linear or melodic sequence and sounded individually. A linear or melodic expression of harmony.

Ascending - moving higher in pitch.

Augmented Chord - a triad with two consecutive major 3rds thus producing a sharp 5 at the 5th of the chord. Augmented 7th chords have an augmented triad and include the mixolydian or lowered 7th. This chord is written as 7#5.

Bar Line - the line that separates measures or bars.

Beat - beat or pulse, the implied and intrinsic foundation of rhythm.

BPM - beats per minute, the speed or tempo at which a piece of music is played that is often expressed as a metronome marking   ex.

Chord - 2 or more notes sounded simultaneously, chords can be played by polyphonic instruments such as piano and guitar but not by monophonic instruments.

Chord Chart - a progression of chords shown with bar lines and sections and often with a tempo indication but without the melody.

Chord Scale - the notes in a scale arranged into a chord and then that chord voicing moves by scale steps throughout the given scale while remaining in the fixed intervallic relationships or specific inversion of that chord. For example 1st inversion triads through the scale of C major.

Chord Spelling - the letter names of the notes of a chord as derived from their parent scale.

Chord Tone - A note that belongs to a chord as opposed to a scale tone which may or may not be part of a chord.

Chromatic Scale - the scale that moves by the smallest increments of a semitone and uses all 12 notes in our system of music including the natural notes and the sharps and flats. It would be the same as playing every key on the piano in succession. (Notes separated by a diagonal line are the same pitch but have a different name, they are called enharmonic)

A - A#/B♭ - B - C - C#/D♭-D - D#/E♭ - E - F - F#/G♭ - G - G#/A♭ - A

Common Finger - a finger that does not have to move when changing from one chord to another.

Compound Interval - an interval that goes past the octave (8) for example a minor 9th or a major 13 or an augmented 11.

Cycle of 5ths - beginning with C and moving in progressive Perfect 5ths through all 12 notes of our chromatic scale. To the right it is the circle of 5ths and to the left its inversion of circle of perfect 4ths. The diagram below also shows the relative minor keys.

Descending - moving lower in pitch.

Diatonic - according to the scale.

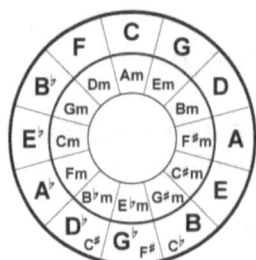

Diminished Chord - (o)- a chord with two consecutive minor 3rds thus producing a flat 5th in the triad.

Diminished 7 Chord (o7) - a diminished triad with an added minor 3rd or diminished 7th from the root, no hierarchical harmonic structure since all the intervals are the same.

Dominant - the perfect 5th degree of a major or minor scale on which the dominant chord is built.

Dominant 7 Chord - the chord built from the V degree or Perfect 5 of a major scale or from the harmonic minor or melodic minor scales. The dominant 7 chord is also referred to as simply the 7 chord and is made up of a major triad with a flat 7 from the tonic.

Double bar line - a double line at the end of a bar that indicates the end of a section. ‖

Double Stop - when two notes are sounded together most often referred to as a double stop in strings literature, violin, viola, cello but is also used to indicate the same technique on the guitar.

Down Beat - - the beats in music that are the pulse or heartbeat of the music, when tapping the foot this downbeat would fall each time the foot touches the floor. Also referred to as beat or pulse, the number of beats or pulses in a measure are indicated as the top number in the time signature.

Duet - two instruments playing together each with their own part.
Ear Training - educating the ear to differentiate between musical sounds and hear critically.

Enharmonic - the same note or pitch with a different name such as Ab and G# or F# and Gb.

Fake Book - a book of songs that are written in a lead sheet style mostly arranged for a maximum of two pages thus negating the necessity of page turns so that the entire piece of music can be read in a live performance context.

Fingering - the physical placement of the fingers of the left hand most often for an optimal and economical result.

First and Second Endings - often sections repeat themselves with a change only in the last 1 or 2 measures. A first ending directs back to the beginning with a repeat and the second time through the second ending provides the alternate ending measure(s). This method provides a more economical way of presenting the musical form.

Flat - the flat sign (♭) lowers a note by a semitone as B to B♭. Lowering a note a semitone moves the note one fret toward the head of the guitar and lowers the pitch.

Fretboard - the hardwood board that is on top of the neck into which the wire frets are inserted.

Frets - referred to as fret I, fret II etc. A fret separates one note from another unlike a violin for instance which has no frets. These fret distances are carefully measured and separated by the fret wire so that the guitar is correctly intonated. An acoustic steel string guitar is typically 14 frets to the body while a classical guitar is 12.

Guide Finger - when changing between two chords this is a finger that is on the same string but a different fret and remains in contact with the string as it slides over the string as if on a rail to the next chord position. This technique is essential to smooth transitions.

Half Diminished - the half diminished triad is a diminished triad with a minor 7th from the root as opposed to the diminished 7th from the root as in the o7. This chord voicing is also called a minor 7 flat 5 - m7♭5 and is the II chord in a minor key.

Half-step - the distance of a semitone

Harmonic - Two or more notes sounded simultaneously. Intervals may be articulated either as harmonic or melodic. Chords articulated as separated notes are called arpeggios, when all the notes are played together and heard together they are called "Harmonic" because they create a harmonic event. The "Harmonic" element in music is often referred to as the vertical because when written the notes are on top of each other vertically and sounded simultaneously. Melody is often referred to as being horizontal. Harmony often supports melody in close relationship.

Harmonic Minor - a Natural Minor scale that raises the 7th degree for harmonic reasons, specifically for the sake of creating a major chord as a dominant chord in a minor key for the purpose of a stronger resolution to the tonic.

Harmonic Overtone Series - the natural laws of acoustical physics that form the basis of tonal music. The Harmonic Overtone Series is the foundation of Music of the Western World. Its effects are as diverse as forming the basis of music theory to the blueprint of the construction of all musical instruments.

Interval - - the distance between two notes

Key - the tonal center to which all other notes in a musical arrangement want to gravitate. The point of resolution also referred to as key or key center.

Key Signature - music uses scales as a template and as a result it becomes more economical to put the sharps and flats of the template scale at the beginning of the piece rather than writing them repeatedly as accidentals throughout the body of a piece.

Lead Sheet - most often a piece of popular music written in a fake book style that includes the melody and chords written over top in a short one page form so that it is easy to read or "fake."

Major Key - a piece of music predominantly using major sounds or tonality rooted in a major scale, being a scale with a major 3rd from the tonic.

Major 3rd - a distance of two tones. The major 3rd is the first interval from the root in a root position major chord.

Major Scale - the most common major scale is Tone, Tone, Semitone, Tone, Tone, Tone, Semitone. The major scale sound will begin with a major 3rd from the root or tonal center. There are other major scale sounds as well such as the Lydian Scale and the Mixolydian scale both of which also have a major 3rd between their tonic and the first third.

Major 7 Chord - a chord with a major triad as its foundation and a major 7th interval from the root to the 7th, the I maj7 chord in the major key. Example:

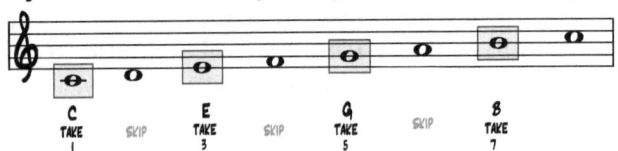

Major Triad - a 3-note chord that has a major 3rd between the root and 3rd giving it a bright sound due to its close proximity to the fundamental in the harmonic overtone series.

Measure - a division of time into measures by using lines and time signatures. in 4/4 time a measure gets 4 beats, in 3/4 a measure gets 3 beats.

Minor Key - a piece of music primarily using minor tonality which would translate to a scale having a minor 3rd from the tonic. Since chords are derived from scales the chords would also exhibit a minor tonality.

Minor 3rd - The distance of a tone plus a semitone, for instance from D to F or G to B♭; D-E-F, 1-2-3, G-A-B♭, 1-2-3. The distance of a minor 3rd is one semitone smaller than a major 3rd. The minor 3rd interval is the 3rd interval from the tonic in a minor scale, chord or key.

Minor Scale - typically a scale with a minor 3rd as its first 3rd interval from the tonic. There are a number of different minor scale sounds such as Natural, Melodic, Harmonic, Dorian, Minor Pentatonic and so on.

Minor 7 Chord - can be built from the II degree of the major scale, minor triad with a minor 7 interval from the root.

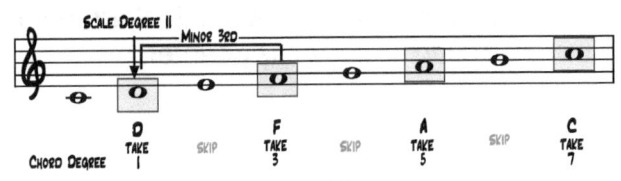

Minor Triad - a 3 note chord with a minor 3rd interval between the root and the 3rd. A darker more complex and melancholic sound than major.

Mixolydian Mode - mode is another word for scale. The mixolydian mode is a common mode that is like the major scale with the exception of having a lowered 7th degree. In the scale of G major the notes are G-A-B-C-D-E-F#-G and in G mixolydian they are G-A-B-C-D-E-F-G without a sharp on the 7th degree. This scale will also produce an F major chord at the 7th degree. There are modes built on every degree of a major scale, these are Ionian, Dorian, Phrygian, Lydian, Mixolydian, Aeolian and Locrian, each will have its own individual sound.

Mode - another word for scale but usually referring to the ecclesiastical modes, each of which can be related to the major scale except starting on different degrees of the scale and each having its own individual arrangement of tones and semitones. Ionian I, Dorian II, Phrygian III, Lydian IV, Mixolydian V, Aeolian VI, Locrian VII.

Muscle Memory - the result of repetition and the central nervous system working together to achieve a subconscious physical result. For example bike riding or swimming or golf or tennis or any other activity requiring immediate responses.

Musical Alphabet - A - B - C - D - E - F - G These letters are used in conjunction with the sharps and flats to give us the 12 notes of our musical system. This same system of letters and sharps and flats is used for all musical instruments and written music in the western world.

Mute - to muffle or dampen.

Natural Minor Scale - - the scale that uses the same notes as its relative minor for example - C major = C - D - E - F - G - A - B - C and its relative Natural minor A Natural Minor - A - B - C - D - E - F - G - A. These scales will sound different because the notes are heard in relation to the tonal centre or key centre, C major = C tonal centre and its relative minor A minor = A tonal centre.

Natural Note - a note without sharps or flats.

Notation - a word for written music, music "notation". Our current system of music notation is the most common and complete method for communicating musical ideas in written form. Our current system has evolved over a thousand years to what it is today.

Note - a musical symbol written on the musical staff that indicates pitch and duration.

Note Value - the length of a note in time.

Octave - the interval distance of eight scale tones from one pitch of the same name to the next pitch of the same name. It is double the frequency or number of vibrations per second. A 110 octave higher A 220 octave higher A 440.

Open String - a string that is not fretted or fingered, it rings as an open note, the open string names are E6, A5, D4, G3, B2, E1.

Parallel - scales that share the same tonal center or tonic, for example C major and C minor would be in parallel, not to be confused with relative which share the same notes.

Perfect Interval - the perfect intervals are perfect unison or P1, perfect octave - P8, perfect 4th - P4 and perfect 5th - P5. Each of these intervals are within the first 3 partials of the harmonic overtone series thus are harmonically pure or perfect.

Pitch - Pitch is closely related to frequency or a number of vibrations or cycles per second but the two are not equivalent. Frequency is an objective, scientific concept, whereas pitch is more subjective and dependent on human interpretation. Sound waves themselves do not have pitch, yet their oscillations can be measured to obtain a frequency. It takes the human mind to map the internal musical quality of pitch. In music pitches are given letter names and then organized and identified in relationships to each other as scales and chords and melodies etc.

Pivot Finger - a finger that is in common between two chords that is kept in place to provide stability in changing from one chord to another.

Position- written in Roman Numerals to indicate the position of the hand, finger 1 aligns with indicated position.

Progression - usually referring to a group of chords that exhibit forward motion and progress one to the next through a pattern of tension and resolution.

Pulse - also known as the beat, the constant and intrinsic yet underlying beat or fixed pulse to which a metronome marking is synchronized to indicate tempo and which is divided to create rhythm.

Relative - sharing the same notes, for example C major and A Natural Minor are relative because they share the same notes. This however does not mean that they are in the same key, in fact C major is the key of C and A minor is the "key" of A minor.

C major - C D E F G A B C   A minor - A B C D E F G A

Relative Key - two scales, chord progressions or musical passages sharing the same notes but in a different key, for example, G major and E minor, C major and D dorian, D major and F# phrygian etc. The notes are the same but the tonal center changes and thus the relationship between the notes changes also.

Repeat Sign - a sign with two bars and two dots that indicates a return to the beginning or to a previous repeat sign.   :||

Rest Stroke - when the pick or finger striking the string comes to rest after the attack on an adjacent string, this for the sake of clarity of technique and beat point.

Root - tonal center, tonic or key center of a scale, chord or piece of music.

Scale - a ladder or template of sonically related notes that move in steps.

Scale Form - A guitarism referring to scale type and fingering.

Semi-tone - the smallest distance in written music notation, for example the distance of C to C# or B to Bb or E to F. Two semitones equals one tone.

Sharp - the sign that raises a note by a semitone. ♯

Sight Reading - the ability to read music at sight on an instrument or with the human voice.
Solo Arrangement - a piece of music arranged to be performed by an unaccompanied instrument.

Staff - The 5 lines and 4 spaces on which music notation is written.

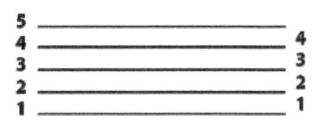

Step - Also known as "whole step" or "whole tone", the distance between two notes consisting of two half steps.

Subdominant - the 4th degree of a major or minor scale that is a perfect 4th away from the tonic on which the subdominant chord is built. It is one of the fundamental chords in the I - IV - V chord progression.

Syncopation - a rhythm that falls primarily off the downbeat and emphasizes the upbeat.

Technique - when used in a musical context it refers to the physical dimension of playing an instrument.

Tempo - speed.

Tertian Harmony - harmony built in thirds, our system of chords is primarily constructed by tertian harmony.

Time Signature - a fraction of two numbers at the beginning of a piece of music that indicates the foundation of time by indicating the number and type of beats in a measure and piece of music. 4/4 = 4 quarter notes per measure, 6/8 = 6 eighth notes per measure etc.

Tonal Centre - synonymous with key center or tonic, rooted in the fundamental of the harmonic overtone series.

Tonality - the general character or color of a piece or passage of music as determined by the choice of key and the relationships between the notes.

Tone - the distance of two semitones.

Tonic - tonal center, key center, root, as related to the fundamental.

Treble Clef - The musical clef that is placed on the staff to indicate where the letter names are placed on the staff, also know as the G clef because it defines that G is on line 2 and the rest of the notes follow in alphabetical sequence.

Triad - a 3 note chord with a root, a third and a fifth.

Tuning - bringing an instrument or voice into pitch with a fixed reference pitch such as a piano or a digital tuner.

Up beat or off beat - the beat that is not the downbeat, music that is predominantly on the up beat is called syncopated.

Voice - a note in a chord having its own characteristics of movement through the process of tension and resolution.

Voicing - the arrangement of the notes in a chord.

WholeTone - the distance of two semitones.

GuitarPal
www.myguitarpal.com

My Guitar Pal is committed to providing an outstanding guitar education experience that leads to a practical and functional understanding of the best instrument on planet earth. Our authors have a combined experience of over a century as educators and performers in a number of styles, and between us we have taught over 100,000 private lessons, played thousands of gigs and recorded in a number of genres. To us the guitar is not a hobby or the corporate corner of a big publishing house - to us the guitar is our art and our passion and it is our desire to share that with you in a way that will not only motivate but will also give you a new insight and creative possibilities on your journey to being the best you can be.

Visit www.MyGuitarPal.com for complete video lessons that support this book and others in the series.

Made in United States
Troutdale, OR
05/13/2024